£1

EX LIBRIS

Molly Kemp

THE LONG CHRISTMAS

The Long Christmas

Stories and carols for Christmas
collected and retold by

RUTH SAWYER

With drawings by

WILLIAM STOBBS

THE BODLEY HEAD
LONDON SYDNEY
TORONTO

ISBN 0 370 01068 X
Printed in Great Britain for
The Bodley Head Ltd
9 Bow Street, London WC2E 7AL
by Unwin Brothers Ltd, Woking
First published by the Viking Press Inc., New York, 1941
First published in Great Britain 1964
Reprinted 1966, 1972

TO PEGGY

This book has been written for my daughter.
I now dedicate it to her, with a sprig of holly,
a sprig of bay, a fat goose, and a tasty plum-pudding,
a tall candle to light and a Yule log to burn
on her hearth the Long Christmas through.

I dedicate it as well to her gift for festival,
to her joy in all small things that mark the
keeping of the season; and especially do I
dedicate it to her gift for telling those
stories of laughter, fancy, and deep feeling which
stir the heart. May these gifts grow and be
abundantly shared throughout the years to come.

CONTENTS

Contents

The Season of the Long Christmas

In planning this book of the *Long Christmas* I have chosen to lengthen the season, as many did in olden times, to last from the first cock-crow on Saint Thomas's Day to the blessing of the candles on Candlemas. It was on Saint Thomas's Day that the poor of city and countryside went a-gooding, or a-mumping, that they might gather in their doles of food and grain against the keeping of Christmas. It was on this day the fiddlers started forth into the street, playing the Christmas in; and the waits with woollen tippets tight about their throats, caps hard over ears, began their carolling. The streets rang with "The Seven Joys of Mary," and "I Saw Three Ships," and "Who Is This and What Is This?" But first and oftenest they sang:

God rest you merry, gentlemen,
Let nothing you dismay,
Remember Christ our Saviour
Was born on Christmas Day,
To save us all from Satan's power
When we were gone astray;
Bringing tidings of comfort and joy.

English chroniclers of the sixteenth century testify to this being the best beloved of all the carols.

Anne Carroll Moore begins her Long Christmas on Saint

Nicholas's Eve. Had I a good story for that night I should begin then, to keep tryst with the Central Children's Room and Miss Moore, sitting with *Knickerbocker* open upon her lap, reading of Oloffe the Dreamer.

It is on Saint Thomas's Day the cooks begin in earnest to string geese and turkeys on the spit, and to dip their plum-puddings. I have always had great respect for those who honour good food; and how can one keep festival without it? More good food, gay and of infinite variety, has been compressed into the Christmas season than into any other. Long before Christ was born peoples celebrated the winter solstice with fires of worship, song, and feasting. The best of the land, in wine and food, was gathered for the Saturnalia and for celebrating the Day of the Great Mother. That feeling for the necessity of good food to make good festival is an ancient one, and still strong within us. The carols sing of it; the ballads list what has been prepared and will be eaten. Ben Jonson presents the most honoured of the Christmas dishes as persons in his *Christmas Masque*.

No people have kept a longer Christmas, or a merrier one, than the English. The wassail bowl belongs to half of Europe, but who has sung of it as the English? The bowl is filled and drained and filled again throughout the season. Herrick has written of it:

Honour to you who sit
Near to the well of it,
And drink your fill of it.

Here is an authentic recipe, found in a seventeenth century manuscript:

> For the brewing let there be ginger, nutmeg, and a pinch of cinnamon. One-half pound of sugar added to some goodly ale, heat, stir, but do not boil. Add a good portion of Malaga wine, the zest of lemon, and six apples cored and roasted.

There is the boar's head, wreathed with holly or bay, an apple or a lemon in its mouth, borne head-high at the beginning of the procession; the plum-pudding at the end, flambé. We have a report that a certain sovereign of England breakfasted Christmas morning on cockles, whiting, plum-porridge, and malmsey. A ballad-maker has sung of the Christmas feast served to the Knights of the Round Table:

> They served up salmon, venison, and wild boars,
> By hundreds and by dozens and by scores.
> Hogsheads of honey, kilderkins of mustard,
>   Muttons and fatted beeves and fatted swine;
> Herons and bitterns, peacocks, swans, and bustards,
>   Teal, mallard, pigeons, widgeons; and in fine
> Plum-puddings, pancakes, apple pies and custard,
>   And washed it down with good Gascon wine.

From *Poor Robin's Almanack* comes:

> Now thrice welcome Christmas
>   Which brings us good cheer,

Mince pies and plum-porridge,
Good ale and strong beer.
With pig, goose, and capon,
The best that can be,
So well doth the weather
And our stomachs agree.

The pastrycooks' windows emptied and filled again before Twelfthnight, when the display reached a splendour well-nigh incredible. The most enchanting cakes appeared! Saint George and the Dragon, stars and knights and horns of plenty, well frosted and stuffed with comfits. When gaffers stood too long outside the window awed with such an exhibition, they had their coat-tails nailed to the framework, or pinned together by the streetboys, to whom such sights were no novelty. In Spain most of the cakes were baked for the Day of the Three Kings in the shape of a fish, the early Christian symbol. And in the Rue des Lombardes in Paris, the confectioners' own street, the windows were filled with coloured sugar in the shape of musical instruments, slippers and boots, pans and pots, all filled with bon-bons.

So much for the feasting. What of the lighting for the Long Christmas? "Thousands of tapers," we read, "filled King Henry's hall at Greenwich." Half the monasteries in Europe, Ireland, and England kept bees, quite as much for the wax they supplied for the candles as for the honey they gathered. The Yule log was lighted on the Eve and kept burning until Twelfthnight, "when a great fire was made of the Christmas greens." There were candles to put in windows to guide the Christ Child; candles to put on trees to blaze through Christmas Night, lighted again for the Eve of the Holy Innocents. On New Year's Eve, or hogmanay, in many countries great fires were built in the orchards or in the fields where grain would be planted. Often there were twelve fires lighted, each named for one of the Apostles. A New Year's wassail was brewed and a libation poured on the earth to ensure a plentiful harvest.

Apple tree, apple tree,
Bear apples for me.
Hats full, caps full,
Sacks full, laps full!

So sang the country children, blowing horns and marching. And again there must be doles for the poor that Christmas may last until Epiphany, when the Three Kings ride.

In England—and the English carried the custom over to the Burgundians—there was always a Prince of Christmas, a Lord of Misrule. Often he was chosen soon after Michaelmas that there might be time aplenty to plan the Christmas revels. He might be courtier, fool, wise man, or beggar, whatever pleased the king's fancy. Feudal lords chose their own Lord of Misrule. Gray's Inn, Oxford, and Cambridge kept the revels. Each Lord or Prince was granted a special purse to defray expenses. Gleemen were hired, costumes made, a new masque written, or a miracle play taken from the old Latin. In kings' courts the Lord of Misrule had an almost unlimited retinue of persons attending him: treasurer, chamberlain, masters of request, mummers, sergeants-at-arms, pages, heralds, trumpeters, jugglers, fools, and friars. Costumes were gaudy, well weighted with mock jewellery, which they called gauds. Some wore antic faces; some came as beasts, as bears to be baited, as lions to perform and dragons to be slain. Madness and merriment; but usually wit was mixed with folly, and reverence with mockery.

Never before within our memory has it seemed so important to keep the Long Christmas; to begin early enough and hold to the festival long enough to feel the deep, moving significance of it. For Christmas is a state of mind quite as much as a festival; and who can establish and maintain a state of mind in the rush and turmoil of a single day, or two days? Around no other time of year has been built so much of faith, of beauty. Out of no other festival have grown so many legends. It is a time when man walks abroad in the full stature of his humanity and in the true image of God. He walks with grace, with laughter, and a great awareness of brotherhood. This bringing of the world together to worship at the manger brings kings and cooks to be in good fellowship, makes children and their grandsires to be of one age, makes witty men of fools and fools of scholars. And who is there to foretell to whom the star may appear?

You will mark that the Devil comes into two of the stories —and a good thing. Is this not a fitting time to remember that never has good ruled the world undisputed? Like that great tide that rises at the equinoxes and so often spreads destruction up and down the Atlantic coast of America, so has evil always risen in cyclic repetition. In olden times, in many a small town and village, it was the custom on Christmas Eve to ring the Old Lad's bell—a way of telling the people that Satan's reign on earth was over, Christ's begun. "Ring out the darkness of the land. Ring in the Christ that is to be." The custom must have continued down to Tennyson's time.

For those who can repeat the genealogy of Jesus on the Eve of Christmas, without hesitation or error, great treasure will be revealed. And in no country is there not some tale told of the Christmas Guest—that holy one—be it Virgin or Child, who, coming along lost, hungry, or cold out of the night, seeks sanctuary. "Who knows," says the old German monk, "that when one opens the door to an unbidden guest on the holy Eve one may not find the Christ." And the people of Donegal even today say: "Forget not the dole to all on the Eve of Saint Stephen; for who can be telling when the Virgin with the new-born Child may come a-hungering to our doors."

The French-Canadian hunters have seen the deer kneel in the forest at midnight on the Eve. In the German Alps the peasants believe all creatures have the gift of human speech and prophecy. In Poland Jacob's Ladder is built again between Earth and Heaven and angels pass freely up and down, ministering to the sick and sad of heart. The gypsies of the Scandinavian countries are forever seeking for that forest where the Christ Child walks at midnight and where a white flower springs up through the frozen earth, wherever His small feet have touched. Trees burst into leaf for the space of that short breath when the Child comes back to earth to remind the world of His birth.

I have a special fondness for the old Rumanian Christmas ballad which tells of Mary spinning cloth for Her Child, spinning fine and soft. She is so proud of Her handiwork, She boasts of it until a small brown spider answers Her and says that she can spin softer and finer than Mary can. Mary chooses Her finest flaxen thread; the spider sets up its web in the corner. It spins gossamer as strong as flax and soft as thistledown. Mary is forced to acknowledge Her defeat; in great anger She bids the spider, all spiders, spin through eternity: "You shall do nothing but spin; and forevermore you shall stay in corners of sheds and barns, while the house shall be forbidden you." It is from this, I judge, that the German legend of the golden cobwebs takes its inception. The Christ Child comes to a farm house on Christmas Eve and finds the house door closed and the spiders waiting outside crying softly together, for they have seen the Christmas tree, cut, but never trimmed. So the Child opens the door and lets them in, bidding them go where they will and see all. This they do, climbing up and over the laden branches of the tree, and, when satisfied, they return to the barn leaving the tree covered with grey web. Knowing the housewife's pride in cleanness and her abhorrence of spiders, the Child blesses the tree and the grey threads covering the branches turn to gold.

In offering this book at this time I feel it is right, perhaps needful, to give more accounting of the inner vision of Christmas, and less of the outer substance. For this reason I have kept almost entirely to legend. In *My Roads* Anne Carroll Moore writes: "We too often forget lighting up time at Christmas and lay upon the day itself too heavy a load of material substitutes for the great good gifts of beauty, song, and laughter, of genuine play and fresh adventure in two worlds."

There are great good gifts to go back to on our bookshelves. Let them not be forgotten. "Dulce Domum" from *The Wind in the Willows;* Dickens's *Magic Fishbone;* Washington Irving's *Old Christmas;* and Anne Carroll Moore's own *Nicholas—A Manhattan Christmas Story.* Especially would I have no family miss reading by fireside Milton's "Hymn to Christ's Nativity." "This is the month, and this the happy morn. . . ." There is in it myrrh and frankincense and gold for the spirit. "And all about the courtly stable bright harnessed angels sit in order serviceable."

Until two thousand years ago the salutation for the winter solstice was: "I give you light for the year." But after Bethlehem the customary salutation became: "I give you Christ —the light of the world."

Ithaca, N. Y. Ruth Sawyer

The Long Christmas of 1941

1. The Shepherds

THE OLDEST LEGEND FROM SPAIN

Words from an Old Spanish Carol

Shall I tell you who will come
to Bethlehem on Christmas Morn,
who will kneel them gently down
before the Lord, new-born?

One small fish from the river,
with scales of red, red gold,
one wild bee from the heather,
one grey lamb from the fold,
one ox from the high pasture,
one black bull from the herd,
one goatling from the far hills,
one white, white bird.

And many children—God give them grace,
bringing tall candles to light Mary's face.

Shall I tell you who will come
to Bethlehem on Christmas Morn,
who will kneel them gently down
before the Lord, new-born?

1. The Shepherds

YOU who keep Christmas, who keep the holy-tide, have you ever thought why a child needs must be born in the world to save it? Here is a Christmas story about God, meaning Good. It begins far back when the world was first created.

In the beginning God had two favourite archangels: one was called Lucifer, meaning Light, and one called Michael, meaning Strength. They led the heavenly hosts; they stood, one on the right hand and one on the left hand of God's throne. They were His chosen messengers.

Now the Archangel Michael served God with his whole heart and angelic soul. There was no task too great for him to perform, no thousand years of service too long. But the Archangel Lucifer chafed at serving any power higher than his own. As one thousand years swept after another thousand years—each as a day—he became bitter in his service and jealous of God.

The appointed time came for God to create the Universe. He made the sun, the moon, the stars. He made earth and water, and separated them. He made trees and flowers and grass to grow; He made creatures to walk the earth and eat thereof; and He made birds for the air and fish for the waters. And when all else was created, He made a man and called him Adam, and a woman and called her Eve. It took Him six heavenly days to create this Universe; and at the end He was tired and rested.

While the Creation was coming to pass and God was occupied most enormously, Lucifer went stealthily about Heaven. He spoke with this angel and with that, whispering, whispering. He spoke with the cherubim and seraphim—to all and everyone who would give him an attending ear. And what he whispered was this: "Why should God rule supreme? Why should He be the only one to create and to say what shall be created? We are powerful. We are worthy to rule. What say you?"

He whispered throughout the six days of Creation; and

when God rested Lucifer led a host of rebellious angels against God; they drew their flaming swords and laid siege to God's throne. But the Archangel Michael drew his flaming sword; he led God's true angels to defend Heaven. The army of Lucifer was put to rout and his captains were taken prisoner and led before God's throne. And God said: "I cannot take life from you, for you are celestial beings. But you shall no longer be known as the hosts of light; you shall be the hosts of darkness. You, Lucifer, shall bear the name of Satan. You and those who have rebelled must seek a kingdom elsewhere. But I command you this—leave this Earth, which I have but freshly made, alone. Molest not my handiwork." So spoke God.

So Lucifer was banished with his minions; and henceforth he was known as Satan. He established a kingdom under the Earth and called it Hell. But because God had commanded him to leave Earth untouched, he straightway coveted Earth for his own. He sent his spirits abroad to tempt and make evil those born upon Earth. So it came to pass that the people of Earth knew at last the power of evil as well as of good; they felt the long reach of darkness even while they lifted their eyes to the Face of Light.

And now the years became millions. Earth became peopled in its four corners; and God looked down upon it and sorrowed. He called Archangel Michael to Him and spoke: "It has come to pass that Satan's power upon Earth is great. No longer can my angels prevail. A kingdom of destruction, of greed, of hate, and of false-witnessing has been set up among my people on the Earth I have created. Their hearts have grown dark with evil; their eyes no longer see the light. I must send to Earth my own spirit that evil may be conquered. He shall be one conceived of Heaven and born of Earth, none less than my own beloved Son." So spoke God.

Earth had been divided into countries, some great and powerful, some small and weak. And the strong reached out even with their armies and took the weak. Now such a one, taken, was called Judea. Within its rolling hills, its olive groves, its high pastures and twisting rivers, men had built a little city called Bethlehem—King David's city. And to this city the conquering Romans had ordered all of the tribe of Jesse to come and render tribute unto Caesar.

Beyond the city, on the high pastures, many shepherds herded their sheep. And it came to pass that God chose Bethlehem to be the place of birth for His Son; and the time to be the taxing time of the year. He chose to reveal the coming to the shepherds, they being men of simple faith and pure hearts. And God sent forth a star to show them the way, and commanded angels to sing to them of the glad tidings.

The night had grown late. High in the pastures the shepherds had built fires to keep themselves warm, to frighten off stray wolves or robbers. All slept but Esteban, the boy. He alone saw the angel, heard the tidings; and straightway he woke the sleeping ones: "Lo, an angel has but now come among us, singing. Wake—wake, all of you! I think this night must have great meaning for us."

Now at this time Satan stood at the gateway of Hell. Of

late he had been troubled in mind, a sense of impending doom moved him. And as he gazed abroad upon the Earth he saw the angel appear. Then did his troubled mind grow fearful. He summoned his hosts of Hell, commanding them to make ready: "Tonight I think again we defy God's power over the Universe. We fight, I think, for Earth, to make it ours. I go to it now. Come when I smite the ground."

Swift as his thought Satan reached the Earth. He came as a wanderer, upon his head a wide sombrero, about his shoulders and falling to the ground a cloak, in his hand a staff. Across the Earth he travelled even as the lightning crosses the sky. He was here—he was beyond. And so he came to the high pastures of Judea and stood at one of the fires about which the shepherds watched. Again the angel came, shouting God's tidings: "Fear not! For unto you is born this day in the city of David a Messiah!"

Satan covered his face and spoke: "What means that message?"

The shepherds cowered. "We know not."

"What is that Saviour—that Messiah yonder apparition shouts of?"

"We know not."

Satan dropped his cloak that they might see the fire that damns and burns shining even in his eyes: "I command you to know!"

It was Benito, the oldest shepherd, who asked: "In the name of God, who are you?"

And Satan answered: "In my own name I am a wanderer.

Once I had taken from me a mighty kingdom. I am here to restore it unto myself."

Could this be the Saviour of whom the angels sang? The shepherds drew close—close. They looked. And to each came terror. Here truly was darkness, not light; here was nameless evil, not good. Here was one who had denied the name of God. Together they shouted: "Begone!" They drew brands from the fire and crossed them, making fiery crosses to burn between themselves and Satan.

While they had been talking among themselves Esteban, the boy, had gone far off seeking stray lambs. Now Satan sought him out. "You heard the angel sing. Where is this City of David?"

"I know not."

"Who is this Messiah?"

"You speak of Matías?" The boy was stupid with fear. "You mean my mother's brother, a shepherd, wise and faithful? But he is ill. I tend his sheep."

"Idiot! Dolt! Fool!" The voice of Satan rose like a whirlwind. "In your great stupidness you sin against me, and that is more terrible than sinning against God. For this you die!"

The boy tried to open his mouth to shriek for mercy. Before words could come, before Satan's hand could smite him, there came between them, out of the vast spaces of the Universe, one who thrust a flaming sword between the Devil and the boy; while through the vast dome of Heaven rang a voice: "Thou shalt not take the innocent!"

It was the voice of the Archangel Michael. He stood now, all in shining armour, beside Esteban, his sword shielding him. And again he spoke: "How dare you break God's command!"

"I dare do more than that." Satan spoke with mockery. "God's Earth is no longer His but mine. My minions rule it. But tonight I shall fight you for it. I shall take it from you by right of sword and mightier hosts."

He stamped the ground. It split asunder, and from its very bowels came forth rank after rank of devils, waving their double-bladed swords forged in Hell's own fires. Then Michael thrust his sword aloft and behold a mighty stairway, even like Jacob's ladder, was built between Earth and Heaven. Down its shining way came rank on rank of the heavenly hosts. Across the sky rang the shout of "Combat!"

Then such a battle was fought between the armies of darkness and the armies of light as had not been waged since the beginning of all things. And Michael's sword pinioned Satan to the ground so that he could not rise; and Michael's hosts put Satan's to rout, so that the Earth's crust broke with them and they were swallowed in belching flames. And when the Earth was rid of them, Michael spoke to Satan: "You have asked of many this night who is the Saviour—the Messiah. I will answer you, defeated. He is God's Son, and Man's. He is Peace. He is Love. He is one against whom your evil cannot prevail. For next to God He is supreme."

The face of Archangel Michael shone with the light of conquering Heaven, all goodness, all strength. And Satan, crawling to his feet, looked upon it and hated it. "I am conquered now. But wait another thousand years, two thousand!"

Meanwhile the boy Esteban watched. And with the crawling of Satan back to Hell, Michael commanded Esteban to lead the shepherds to Bethlehem that they might look upon the face of their Saviour, and worship Him.

And as the boy joined the shepherds about their fires, there came the angel again, the third time; and with it was a multitude of the heavenly host, praising God and singing hallelujahs! While over all shone a star of a magnitude never seen by them before in all the heavens.

But of the many watching their flocks that night only a few heeded. These wrapped their cloaks about them and followed the boy Esteban. As they walked he pointed out the roadsides, guarded by rank on rank of angels in shining armour. But none saw them save the boy.

Yet a great joy welled up in each heart, so that every shepherd needs must raise his voice in song. Benito, the oldest, gave them words for the beginning:

Yonder star
in the skies
marks the manger
where He lies.

Then Andrés caught the air and gave them the second verse to sing:

The Shepherds

Joy and laughter,
  song and mirth
herald in
  our Saviour's birth.

Miguel lifted his voice in a great swelling tumult of thanksgiving:

Now good will
  unto all men.
Shout it, brothers,
  shout again!

Carlos caught from him the song and threw it back to the others with gladness:

Peace then be
  among us all;
upon great nations
  and on small!

It was Esteban who gave the words for the last, singing them down the end of the road, leading them to the stable opening:

Let each shepherd
  raise his voice
till the whole world
  shall rejoice;
till in one voice

all shall sing—
Glory to our
Saviour—King!

The star overhead lighted the way into the stable. Within they found a young woman, very fair, and on the straw beside her a small, new-born child. Benito spoke the questions that were in the minds of all: "What is thy name, woman?"

"They call me Mary."

"And his—the child's?"

"He is called Jesus."

Benito knelt. "*Nene Jesús*—Baby Jesus, the angels have sent us to worship thee. We bring what poor gifts are ours. Here is a young cockerel for thee." Benito laid it on the straw beside the child, then rose and called: "Andrés, it is thy turn."

Andrés knelt. "I, Andrés, bring thee a lamb." He put it with the cockerel, rose, and said: "Miguel, give thine."

Miguel knelt. "I bring thee a basket of figs, little one. Carlos, thy turn."

Carlos knelt and held out shepherd-pipes. "I have made them. Thou shalt play on them when thou art grown. Juan, what hast thou?"

Juan knelt. "Here is some cheese—good goats' cheese."

In turn they knelt, each shepherd, until all but Esteban, the boy, had given his gift. "Alas, *Nene Jesús,* I have little for thee. But here are the ribbons from my cap. Thou likest them, yes? And now I make a prayer: 'Bless all shepherds.

Give us to teach others the love for all gentle and small things that is in our hearts. Give us to see thy star always on this, the night of thy birth. And keep our eyes lifted eternally to the far hills.' "

And having made the prayer, and all having given their gifts, the shepherds departed into the night, singing.

2. Fiddler, Play Fast, Play Faster

A DANSE MACABRE FROM THE ISLE OF MAN

The Seven Joys of Mary

[A begging song to be sung on Saint Thomas's Day]

The first good joy that Mary had was having Him a little lad
To suckle at Her breast.
The second joy—let angels sing—was the Three Kings come worshipping
Before the manger blest.
The next good joy, which numbered three, was when He made the blind to see,
And sent them whole away.
The fourth good joy, Him we adore, He taught the priests by the temple door,
Departing then to pray.
The next good joy, which numbereth five, behold the dead is now alive,
And walketh from the tomb.
The sixth good joy—let sinners all repent their sins both great and small
And so escape their doom.
The last good joy—the joy of seven—Lord Jesus wears the crown of Heaven;
In Heaven Lord Jesus doth abide; so give us dole this holy-tide.

2. Fiddler, Play Fast, Play Faster

IT is a strange island and an enchanted one—our Isle of Man. It took many a thousand years and more before mankind discovered it, it being well-known that the spirits of water, of earth, of air and fire did put on it an enchantment, hiding it with a blue flame of mist, so that it could not be seen by mortal eye. The mist was made out of the heat of a great fire and the salt vapour of the sea and it covered the island like a bank of clouds. Then one day the fire was let out, the sea grew quiet, and lo, the island stood out in all its height of mountains and ruggedness of coast, its green of fens and rushing of waterfalls. Sailors passing saw it. And from that day forth men came to it and much of its enchantment was lost.

But not all. Let you know that at all seasons of the year there are spirits abroad on the Isle, working their charms and making their mischief. And there is on the coast, overhanging the sea, a great cavern reaching below the earth, out of which the Devil comes when it pleases him, to walk where he will upon the Isle. A wise Manxman does not go far without a scrap of iron or a lump of salt in his pocket; and if it is night, likely, he will have stuck in his cap a sprig of rowan and a sprig of wormwood, feather from a seagull's wing and skin from a conger eel. For these keep away evil spirits; and who upon the Isle would meet with evil, or who would give himself foolishly into its power?

So it is that in the south upon the ramparts of Castle Rushen the cannon are mounted on stone crosses above the ramparts; and when a south Manxman knocks at his neighbour's door he does not cry out: "Are you within?" But rather he asks: "Are there any sinners inside?" For evil is a fearsome thing, and who would have traffic with it?

I am long at beginning my tale, but some there may be who know little of our Isle and a storyteller cannot always bring his listeners by the straightest road to the story he has to tell. This one is of the south, where the mists hang the heaviest, where the huts are built of turf and thatched with broom, where the cattle are small and the goats many, and where a farmer will tell you he has had his herd brought to fold by the fenodyree—a goblin that is half goat, half boy. But that is another tale.

Let me begin with an old Manx saying—it tunes the story well: "When a poor man helps another, God in His Heaven laughs with delight." This shows you that the men of Man are kind to one another, and God is not far from them even when the Devil walks abroad.

Count a hundred years, and as many more as you like, and you will come to the time of my story. Beyond Castletown in the sheading of Kirk Christ Rushen lived, then, a lump of a lad named Billy Nell Kewley. He could draw as sweet music from the fiddle as any fiddler of Man. When the Christmas-time began, he was first abroad with his fiddle. Up the glens and over the fens, fiddling for this neighbour and that as the night ran out, calling the hour and crying the weather, that those snug on their beds of chaff would know before the day broke what kind of day it would be making. Before Yule he started his fiddling, playing half out of the night and half into the day, playing this and playing that, carrying with him, carefully in his cap, the sprig of rowan and the sprig of wormwood, with the iron and salt in the pocket of his brown woollen breeches. And there you have Billy Nell Kewley on the Eve of Saint Fingan.

Now over Castletown on a high building of cliff rises Castle Rushen. Beyond stands the oldest monastery on the Isle, in ruin these hundreds of years, Rushen Abbey, with its hundred treens of land. It was through the Forest of Rushen Billy Nell was coming on Saint Thomas's Eve, down the Glen to the Quiggan hut, playing the tune "Andisop" and whistling a running of notes to go with it. He broke the whistle, ready to call the hour: "Two of the morning," and the weather: "Cold—with a mist over all," when he heard the running of feet behind him in the dark.

Quick as a falcon he reached for the sprig in his cap. It was gone; the pushing through the green boughs of the forest had torn it. He quickened his own feet. Could it be a buggan after him—an ugly, evil one, a fiend of Man who cursed mortals and bore malice against them, who would bring a body to perdition and then laugh at him? Billy Nell's feet went fast—went faster.

But his ear, dropping behind him, picked up the sound of other feet; they were going fast—and faster. Could it be the fenodyree—the hairy one? That would be not so terrible. The fenodyree played pranks, but he, having once loved a human maid, did not bring evil to humans. And he lived, if the ancient ones could be believed, in Glen Rushen.

And then a voice spoke out of the blackness. "Stop, I command!"

What power lay in that voice! It brought the feet of Billy Nell to a stop—for all he wanted them to go on, expected them to keep running. Afterwards he was remembering the salt and iron in his pocket he might have thrown between himself and what followed so closely after him out of the mist. But he did nothing but stop—stop and say to himself:

"Billy Nell Kewley, could it be the Noid ny Hanmey who commands—the Enemy of the Soul?" And he stood stock still in the darkness too frightened to shiver, for it was the Devil himself he was thinking of.

He who spoke appeared, carrying with him a kind of reddish light that came from everywhere and nowhere, a light the colour of fever, or heat lightning, or of the very pit of Hell. But when Billy Nell looked he saw as fine a gentleman as ever had come to Man—fine and tall, grave and stern, well clothed in knee breeches and silver buckles and lace and such finery. He spoke with grace and grimness: "Billy Nell Kewley of Castletown, I have heard you are a monstrous good fiddler. No one better, so they say."

"I play fair, sir," said Billy Nell modestly.

"I would have you play for me. Look!" He dipped into a pocket of his breeches and drawing out a hand so white, so tapering, it might have been a lady's, he showed Billy Nell gold pieces. And in the reddish light that came from everywhere and nowhere Billy saw the strange marking on them. "You shall have as many of these as you can carry away with you if you will fiddle for me and my company three nights from tonight," said the fine one.

"And where shall I fiddle?" asked Billy Nell Kewley.

"I will send a messenger for you, Billy Nell; half-way up the Glen he will meet you. This side of midnight he will meet you."

"I will come," said the fiddler, for he had never heard of so much gold—to be his for a night's fiddling. And being not half so fearful he began to shiver. At that moment a cock crew far away, a bough brushed his eyes, the mist hung about him like a cloak, and he was alone. Then he ran, ran to Quiggan's hut, calling the hour: "Three of the clock," crying the weather: "Cold, with a heavy mist."

The next day he counted, did Billy Nell Kewley, counted the days up to three and found that the night he was to fiddle for all the gold he could carry with him was Christmas Eve. A kind of terror took hold of him. What manner of spirit was the Enemy of the Soul? Could he be anything he chose to be—a devil in Hell or a fine gentleman on Earth? He ran about asking everyone, and everyone gave him a different answer. He went to the monks of the Abbey and found them working in their gardens, their black cowls thrown back from their faces, their bare feet treading the brown earth.

The Abbot came, and dour enough he looked. "Shall I go, your reverence? Shall I fiddle for one I know not? Is it good gold he is giving me?" asked Billy Nell.

"I cannot answer any one of those questions," said the Abbot. "That night alone can give the answers: Is the gold good or cursed? Is the man noble or is he the Devil? But go. Carry salt, carry iron and bollan bane. Play a dance and watch. Play another—and watch. Then play a Christmas hymn and see!"

This side of midnight, Christmas Eve, Billy Nell Kewley climbed the Glen, his fiddle wrapped in a lamb's fleece to keep out the wet. Mist, now blue, now red, hung over the blackness, so thick he had to feel his way along the track with his feet, stumbling.

He passed where Castle Rushen should have stood. He passed on, was caught up and carried as by the mist and in it. He felt his feet leave the track, he felt them gain it again. And then the mist rolled back like clouds after a storm and before him he saw such a splendid sight as no lump of a lad had ever beheld before. A castle, with courtyard and corridors, with piazzas and high roofings, spread before him all a-glowing with light. Windows wide and doorways wide, and streaming with the light came laughter. And there was his host more splendid than all, with velvet and satin, silver and jewels. About him moved what Billy Nell took to be highborn lords and ladies, come from overseas no doubt, for never had he seen their like on Man.

In the middle of the great hall he stood, unwrapping his fiddle, sweetening the strings, rosining the bow, limbering his fingers. The laughter died. His host shouted:

"Fiddler, play fast—play faster!"

In all his life and never again did Billy Nell play as he played that night. The music of his fiddle made the music of a hundred fiddles. About him whirled the dancers like crazy rainbows: blue and orange, purple and yellow, green and red all mixed together until his head swam with the colour. And yet the sound of the dancers' feet was the sound of the grass growing or the corn ripening or the holly reddening—which is to say no sound at all. Only there was the sound of his playing, and above that the sound of his host shouting, always shouting:

"Fiddler, play fast—play faster!"

Ever faster—ever faster! It was as with a mighty wind Billy Nell played now, drawing the wild, mad music from his fiddle. He played tunes he had never heard before, tunes which cried and shrieked and howled and sighed and sobbed and cried out in pain.

"Play fast—play faster!"

He saw one standing by the door—a monk in a black cowl, barefooted, a monk who looked at him with deep, sad eyes and held two fingers of his hand to his lips as if to hush the music.

Then, and not till then, did Billy Nell Kewley remember what the Abbot had told him. But the monk—how came he here? And then he remembered that, too. A tale so old it had grown ragged with the telling, so that only a scrap here and there was left: how long ago, on the blessed Christmas Eve, a monk had slept through the Midnight Mass to the Virgin and to the new-born Child, and how, at complin on Christmas Day, he was missing and never seen again. The ancient ones said that the Devil had taken him away, that Enemy of All Souls, had stolen his soul because he had slept over Mass.

Terror left Billy Nell. He swept his bow so fast over the strings of his fiddle that his eyes could not follow it.

"Fiddler, play fast—play faster!"

"Master, I play faster and faster!" He moved his own body to the mad music, moved it across the hall to the door where stood the monk. He crashed out the last notes; on the floor at the feet of the monk he dropped iron, salt, and bollan bane. Then out of the silence he drew the notes of a Christmas carol—softly, sweetly it rose on the air:

Adeste fideles, laeti triumphantes,
Venite, venite in Bethlehem:
Natum videte, Regem angelorum:
Venite adoremus, venite adoremus,
Venite adoremus—Dominum.

Racked were the ears of Billy Nell at the sounds which surged above the music, groans and wailing, the agony of souls damned. Racked were his eyes with the sights he saw: the servants turned to fleshless skeletons, the lords and ladies to howling demons. And the monk with the black cowl and bare feet sifted down to the grass beneath the vanishing castle—a heap of grey dust. But in the dust shone one small spark of holy light—a monk's soul, freed. And Billy Nell took it in his hand and tossed it high in the wind as one tosses a falcon to the sky for free passage. And he watched it go its skimming way until the sky gathered it in.

Billy Nell Kewley played his way down the Glen, stopping to call the hour: "Three of this blessed Christmas Morning," stopping to cry the weather: "The sky is clear . . . the Christ is born."

3. The Wee Christmas Cabin of Carn-na-ween

THEY TELL IT STILL IN IRELAND

A Cabin Cradle Song

Hush, *mo croidhe,* hush,
The birds are asleep in the brush;
The stars are crowding the sky wi' their light
As they did long ago on Nativity Night.
Hush, *mo croidhe,* hush.

Sleep, *mo croidhe,* sleep.
Each hill holds its full o' white sheep.
Three Kings on their camels wi' treasure I see,
But love is the birth-gift my heart brings to ye.
Sleep, *mo croidhe,* sleep.

Rest, *mo croidhe,* rest.
Each mother that beareth is blest.
Hark, Mother Mary, look down as I pray,
And bless ye all childher at this ring o' day.
Rest, *mo croidhe,* rest.

3. The Wee Christmas Cabin of Carn-na-ween

A HUNDRED years ago and more, on a stretch of road that runs from the town of Donegal to Killybegs and the sea, a drove of tinkers went their way of mending pots and thieving lambs. Having a child too many for the caravan they left it, new-born, upon a cabin doorsill in Carn-na-ween.

The cabin belonged to Bridget and Conal Hegarty. Now these two had little wish for another child, having childher aplenty of their own; but they could not leave the wee thing to die at their door, nor had they a mind to throw it into the turf-pit. So Bridget suckled it with her own wean; she divided the cradle between them. And in time she came to love it as her own and fought its battles when the neighbours would have cursed it for a tinker's child.

I am forgetting to tell you that the child was a girl and Bridget named her Oona. She grew into the prettiest, the gentlest-mannered lass in all the county. Bridget did her best to get the lads to court her, forever pointing out how clever she was with her needle, how sweet her voice when she lilted an air, the sure way she had of making bannock, broth, or jam.

But the lads would have none of her. Marry a tinker's child? Never! Their feet might be itching to take her to a cross-road's dance, their arms hungering to be holding her, but they kept the width of a cabin or the road always between her and them. Aye, there was never a chance came to Oona to marry and have childher of her own, or a cabin she could call hers.

All of Bridget's and Conal's lasses married; but Oona stayed on to mind the house for them, to care for them through their sicknesses, to help them gently into their graves. I think from the beginning Oona had a dream—a dream that, having cared lovingly for the old, someone would be leaving her at long last a cabin for her own keeping. Bridget, before she died, broke the dream at its beginning. "The cabin goes to Michael," she said. "He and his young wife will not be wanting ye, I'm thinking. Go to the chest and take your share of the linen. Who knows but some man, losing his wife, will be glad to take ye for his second. I'd not have ye going empty-handed to him."

Oona held fast to the dream; she let neither years nor heart-aches shatter it. There was always a cabin waiting to welcome her as soon as another had finished with her. From the time when Oona left the Hegarty cabin, a bonny lass still, with strength to her body and laughter in her eyes, to the time when she was put out of the MacManuses', old and with little work left in her, the tale runs thin as gossamer. But if you are knowing Ireland and the people of Donegal it is not hard to follow the tinker's child through that running of years.

From cabin to cabin, wherever trouble or need abided, there went Oona. In a cabin where the mother was young, ailing, with her first-born, there you would find Oona caring for the child as it had been her own. In a cabin where the childher had grown and gone dandering off to Belfast, Dublin, or America and left the old ones behind, there she tended them as she would have tended her own had she ever known them. In a cabin where a man had lost his wife and was ill-fitted to mind the house and the weans alone—aye, here she was the happiest. She would be after taking over the brood as a mother would, gentling the hurt that death had left behind, and for herself building afresh the dream.

But her birth betrayed her at every turn of the road. No

man trusted her to be his first or second wife. Not one of the many she served and loved guessed of the hunger that grew with the years for a cabin she could call hers. All blessed her name while she lived; and for the hundred years since she has been gone from Carn-na-ween the tales about her have been kept green with loving memory. Those she served saw that she never went empty-handed away. So to Bridget Hegarty's linen was added a griddle, pans, kettles, crocks, creels, and dishes.

Each thing she chose from the cabin she was leaving was something needed to make the home she dreamed of gay and hold comfort. As the years went by, the bundle of her possessions grew, even as she dwindled. Men, women, and childher who passed her on the road at such times as she might be changing cabins would stop to blather with her. Pointing to the size of her bundle they would say: " 'Tis twice your size, the now. Ye'll have to be asking for oxen and a cart to fetch it away from the next cabin." And they would laugh. Or they would say: "Ye might be asking the Marquis to build ye a castle next his own. Ye'll be needing a fair-sized place to keep all ye've been gathering these many years."

Always she would blather back at them. For all her dream was dimming she was never one to get down-daunted. "Ye can never be telling," she would say, "I may yet be having a wee cabin of my own some day. I'm not saying how and I'm not saying when." And she would nod her head in a wise, knowledgeable way, as if she could look down the nose of the future and see what was there.

She was in the cabin of the MacManuses' when the great famine came. The corn in the fields blighted; the potatoes rotted in the ground. There was neither food for man nor fodder for beast. Babies starved at their mothers' breasts, strong men grew weak as childher, dragging themselves into the fields to gnaw at the blistered grass and die under a cruel, drouthing sun. Everywhere could be heard the crying of childher and the keening for the dead. At the beginning neighbour shared with neighbour until death stalked them. Then it was every cabin for itself, and many a man sat all night, fowling-piece across his knee, to keep guard over a last cow in the byre or the last measure of meal in the bin.

So old had Oona grown by famine-time that the neighbours had lost all count of her years. She moved slowly on unsteady feet. Her eyes were dulled; her speech was seldom coming now. But for all that she was worth the sheltering and the scanty food she ate. She milked, she churned, she helped the oldest lad carry the creel to the bog, she helped at the cutting of the turf. So long as there was food enough for them the MacManuses kept her and blessed the Virgin for another pair of hands to work.

But famine can put stones in the place of human hearts, and hunger can make tongues bitter. As the winter drew in, Oona for all her dullness saw the childher watching every morsel of food she put to her lips. She heard the mother's tongue sharpen as she counted out the spoonfuls of stirabout that went into the bowls. Harvest had come and gone, and there was no harvest. The cold, cruel winds of

December rattled at their doors and windows. Of one thing only was there enough: there was always turf in the bog to cut, to dry, to keep the hearth warm.

The childher in the cabin cried from cock-crow till candle-time. Oona wished her ears had been as dulled as her eyes. But for all that she closed her heart to the crying, telling herself she had earned what little food she took, and the good heat for her old body. But a night came when she could stand the crying no longer, when the spoon scraped the bottom of the meal-bin, when the last of the praties had been eaten, their skins with them.

Saying never a word she got up at last from the creepie where she had been thawing her bones and started to put together again her things into her bundle. The MacManuses watched her, and never a word said they. The corners of the great cloth were tied at last. Over her bent shoulders Oona laid her shawl. The cabin was quiet the now, the childher having cried themselves asleep with hunger. Oona dragged her bundle to the door; as she lifted the latch she spoke:

"Ye can fend for yourselves. Ye'll not want me the now."

"Aye, 'tis God's truth." It was the wife who said it.

Timothy MacManus reached for her hand: "Hush, are ye not remembering what night it is?"

"Aye, 'tis Christmas Eve. What matter? There be's not sense enough left in the old one's mind to know it. And in times such as these there is naught to put one night ahead of another."

" 'Twill be a curse on us, the same, if we let her go."

" 'Twill be a curse on her if she stays."

"God and Mary stay with ye, this night," Oona called, going out the door.

"God and Mary go with ye," the two mumbled back at her.

Outside Oona lifted the bundle to her back. How she had strength for this I cannot be telling you. It often comes, a strange and great strength, to those who have borne much and have need to bear more. Oona took the road leading to Killybegs and the sea. A light snow was falling and the wind had dropped to a low whispering. As she went down the village street she stopped to glimpse each cabin and the lighted room within. Hardly a cabin but she had lived in; hardly a face but she had read long and deeply over many years. Her lips made a blessing and a farewell for every door she passed.

All cabins were left behind as the road grew steeper. She climbed with a prayer on her lips—what prayer I do not know, but it lightened the load she carried on her back and in her heart, it smoothed the roughness of her going. She came at last to the bogland. It stretched on and on beyond the reach of eye, even in the daylight. In the dark she sensed only a levelling off, where feet could rest. She stumbled from the road and found shelter under a blackthorn which grew on the fringe of the bog.

"I like it here," she said as she eased the bundle from her back. "Always, I have liked it here. Many's the time I have said: some day I will take the whole of it and climb the hill and sit under this very thorn, the way I'll be feeling the wind from the sea and watching the sun set on it, and the stars lighting it; and, mayhap, hearing the sound of fairy pipes. I never came; I never had the day whole."

She said it in a kind of wonder. She was safe here from the reach of neighbours. It was in her heart that she could never again bear to have man or woman offer her food needed for young mouths. Too many times she had folded tired hands; too many times she had shut weary eyes, not to know what a gentle companioning death could give the old at the end. " 'Tis a friend, he is, that I have known long. 'Tis as a friend he will be coming, calling softly, wishfully: 'Come, Oona!' "

After that her head grew light. She lost all count of time; she lost all track of space. She felt no cold, no tiredness. She could gather years into her mind as cards into the hand, shuffle them about and draw out the ones she liked best. She remembered suddenly that one of the reasons for wanting to climb the hill was to find the fairy rath that lay somewhere along the bog. Conall of a Thousand Songs had slept a Midsummer Night with his head to this rath and had wakened in the morning with it filled full of fairy music—music of enchantment. Wully Donoghue had crossed the rath late one May Eve and caught the fairy host riding abroad. Many a time, herself, she had put a piggin of milk with a bowl of stirabout on the back steps of those cabins she had lived in, remembering how well the Gentle People liked milk and stirabout. Aye, the Gentle People, the Good People! She hoped famine had not touched them. It would be a sorry thing to have the fairy folk starved off the earth.

She slept a little, woke, and slept again. Above the sleeping her mind moved on a slow current. Snow had covered her, warm. This was Christmas Eve, the time of the year when no one should go hungry, no one cold. It would be a white Christmas on the morrow, and the people of Donegal had a saying that when a white Christmas came the Gentle People left their raths and trooped abroad to see the wonder of it. Aye, that was a good saying. They would make good company for a lonely old woman.

Her legs were cramping under her. She strove to move them, and as she did so she had a strange feeling that she had knocked something over. Her old eyes peered into the darkness, her hand groped for whatever it was she had upset. To her amazement when she held her hand under her eyes there was a fairy man, not a hand high. His wee face was puckered with worry. "Don't ye be afeard, wee man," she clucked to him. "I didn't know ye were after being where ye were. Was there anything at all ye were wanting?"

"Aye, we were wanting ye."

"Me!"

"None else. Look!"

And then she saw the ground about her covered with hundreds upon hundreds of Gentle People, their faces no bigger round than buttons, all raised to hers, all laughing.

"What might ye be laughing at?" she asked. "Tell me, for it be's a lee long time since I had laughter on my own lips."

"We are laughing at ye, tinker's child. Living a lifetime in other folks' cabins, serving and nursing and mothering and loving, and never a cabin or kin ye could call your own."

"Aye," she sighed, "aye, 'tis the truth."

" 'Tis no longer the truth. Bide where ye be, Oona Hegarty, and sleep the while."

She did as she was bidden but sleep was as thin as the snow which covered her, breaking through in this place and that, so that she might see through it what was going on about her. Hither and yon the Good People were hurrying. They brought stones, they brought turf. They laid a roof-tree and thatched it. They built a chimney and put in windows. They hung a door at the front and a door at the back. As they worked they sang, and the song they made drifted into Oona's sleep and stayed with her:

'Tis a snug Christmas cabin we're building the night,
    That we're building the night.
The stones make the walls and the turf chinks it tight,
    Aye, the turf chinks it tight.
There'll be thatch for the roof to keep wind out and rain,
    To keep wind out and rain.
And a fire on the hearth to burn out all pain,
    Aye, burn out all pain.
The meal in the chest will stand up to your chin,
    Well up to your chin;

There'll be Christmas without, and Christmas within,
Always Christmas within.
There'll be plenty of currants, and sugar, and tea,
Aye, plenty of tea;
With the chintz at the windows as gay as can be,
All as gay as can be.

There was more to the song. It went on and on, and Oona could not tell where the song ended and the dream began, so closely woven were the two together. She felt of a sudden a small, tweaking hand on her skirt and heard a shrill voice piping: "Wake up—wake up, Oona Hegarty!"

" 'Tis awake I am, entirely," said Oona, sitting up and rubbing her eyes. "Awake and dreaming at the same time, just."

"We'll be after fetching in your bundle, then; and all things shall find their rightful places at last."

Ten hundred fairy men lifted the bundle and bore it inside, with Oona following. She drew her breath through puckered lips; she let it out again in sighs of wonderment. "Is everything to your liking, ma'am?" inquired the fairy man she had knocked over.

She made the answer as she looked about her: "The bed's where it should be. The chintz now—I had a mind to have it green, with a touch of the sun and a touch of the flaming turf in it. The dresser is convenient high. Wait till I have my bundle undone and the treasures of a lifetime put away."

The Gentle People scuttled about helping her, putting the linen in the fine oak chest, the dishes on the dresser.

The kettle was hung above the hearth, the creepie put beside it. The rug spread along the bedside and the griddle left standing by the fire, ready. All things in their right places, as the tinker's child had dreamed them.

"Is it all to your liking?" shouted the Gentle People together.

"Aye, 'tis that and more. Crocks and creels where they do belong. The fine, strong spoon to be hanging there, ready to stir the griddle-bread. The knife with the sharp edge to it, to be cutting it." She turned and looked down at the floor, at the hundreds of wee men crowding her feet: "I'm not asking why ye have done this thing for me this night. But I ask one thing more. On every white Christmas let you be bringing folk to my door—old ones not needed longer by others, children crying for their mother—a lad or a lass for whom life has gone amiss. Fetch them that I may warm them by the hearth and comfort them."

"We will do that, tinker's child; we will do that!" The voices of the Gentle People drifted away from her like a wind dying over the bog: it was there—it was gone. A great sleep took Oona Hegarty so that her eyes could stay open no longer. She put herself down on the out-shot bed. She pulled the warm blanket over her and drew the chintz curtains.

The next night—Christmas—hunger drove Maggie, the middle child of the MacManuses', out of their cabin. She went like a wee wild thing, knowing only the hunger-pain she bore and the need of staying it. Blindly she climbed the hill to the bogland. Weak and stumbling she was, whimpering like a poor, hurt creature. She stumbled off the road, she stumbled over the sudden rise on the bog which nearly laid her flat. Rubbing her eyes she looked up at a wee cabin standing where no cabin had ever been. Through the windows came a welcoming light. In wonderment she lifted the latch and went in.

"Come in, Maggie, I've been looking for ye, the lee long day." It was Oona's voice that spoke to her; aye, but what a changed Oona! She knelt by the hearth turning the griddle-bread, her eyes as blue as fairy-thimbles, her hair the colour of ripened corn. There were praties boiling in the kettle, tea making on the hearth. Enough to eat and to spare. But that was not what filled the child's eyes with wonder. It was Oona herself, grown young, with the look of a young bride on her. "Take the creepie." Her voice had the low, soft calling of a throstle to its young. "Ye'll be after eating your fill, Maggie, and not knowing hunger again for many a day."

And it's the truth I am telling. Maggie went back and told; but although half of Carn-na-ween hunted the cabin throughout the year none found it. Not until a white Christmas again came round. Then old Seumus MacIntyre the cobbler died, leaving his widow Molly poor and none to keep her. They were coming to fetch her to the workhouse that Christmas Eve when she took the road climbing to Killybegs and the sea, and was never seen again.

And so the tales run. There are enough to be filling a book, but why should I go on with them? You can be after telling them to yourselves. This I know: given a white Christmas this year the wee fairy cabin of Carn-na-ween will be having its latch lifted through the night by the lone and the lost and the heart-broken. Aye, Oona Hegarty, the tinker's child, will be keeping the griddle hot, the kettle full, and her arms wide to the childher of half the world this night—if it be's a white Christmas.

4. The Good Night

TOLD BY THE FINNISH GYPSIES

A Gypsy Song of the Road

Long, dark road, long, weary trail,
Shorten it, rom, with a Christmas tale;

With a Christmas tale of the Little King's birth,
When carolling stars looked down on the earth.

Tired horses and tired men
Listen for the angels' song again;

Listen for Hosannas to fill the sky
While the night's dark road goes winding by.

Hungry children, fallen asleep.
What of the shepherds and the watch they keep?

Who will be first to reach the manger?
Who look first on the new-born stranger?

Heavy wheels turn; reins hang slack;
Nell with her Bill and Jo with her Jack;

Eyes turned heavenwards, waiting to hear
The stars tell again what they saw that year.

That year of Christmas when Little King was born,
When Orion shouted it from his seat at dawn;

When the roms from Egypt travelled the world over,
Searching for the stable wherein lay their Saviour.

Long, dark road, long, weary way,
Campfires lighted at the end of the day.

Christ candle burning, wine to bless the sod;
Lift a cup to Little King, Mary and God.

4. The Good Night

DO you still remember the story of the Good Night? There is only one good night in the long space of a year and that is Christmas Night. Of that night we know many tales. Every night the angels watch over good children, but there is not peace on every night. There is only one night of peace when the whole earth worships and prays to God. Then none shall talk evil of another.

There was once a wonderful expectation in the world. All knew that a new and great thing was to happen, but none knew what it was. The stars in the sky looked questioningly at one another.

"What is it?" asked Capella on the right side of the sky to Aldebaran on the left.

White rays flew to and fro; but Aldebaran answered quietly and secretly: "Sister, I do not know."

Vega in the northern sky asked Sirius in the lower sky: "When will this wonderful thing come to pass?"

But Sirius did not know *when,* and Aldebaran did not know *what.*

The stars on the side travelled around the Northern Star and they thought every time they passed: "This time will this new thing come into the world?" But a thousand years went by and no new thing happened.

Now in Bethlehem of Judea there lived a donkey driver who had grown rich. He had built himself a resting place for travellers; these rooms he let out to the rich; the poor could sleep where they found room to lay their heads. A great census and paying of taxes were to be taken where each would enrol himself for numbering in his own city; and as Bethlehem was King David's city the donkey driver knew that many would come there, and so he would make much money. Many came; all his rooms were taken except one—the finest and the best. This one he saved for a prince.

"Look!" shouted Capella across the sky to Aldebaran. "There are many people passing and repassing over the face of the earth. Can this great thing now be about to happen?"

And Aldebaran answered secretly and quietly: "Sister, I do not know."

Now there came to Bethlehem from Nazareth a carpenter, leading a donkey upon which sat a woman. He led it to the place kept by the donkey driver and found the yard outside crowded, many covering the ground. He went to the door and spoke: "Outside there waits one who is my wife. She has come far; she is spent; and this night she must have a place that is her own."

But the donkey driver could see nothing but poorness about the carpenter, and the room that was left was the best. It must be kept for a rich one, a prince. So he said: "There is still room on the ground."

But he had two children—a boy and a girl, kind children. They were holding the donkey on which the woman sat and they were wishing that their father would give the best place to her. Looking into her face, they found it lovely and there was something strange and altogether wonderful in her smile. For her the place seemed none too good. They heard what the father said to the carpenter, and they felt very sorry and looked one at the other. "There is the cave—our father stables his donkeys there," they said. "It is dry, and there is shelter from the wind. Also much hay. It is better than the ground. We will show you."

And the woman smiled and laid her hand over theirs; and they led the donkey, the carpenter following. "King David slept often in caves. We are thankful for a resting place like this," he said. The children made the woman comfortable, spreading much hay between the mangers. "Sleep in peace," they said. And the woman answered them, smiling: "Sleep ye in peace."

Up in the sky a great star was blazing, which had never been there before. A thousand, thousand stars were lost in wonder at it. Regulus shouted to the king star, Orion: "What does it mean?"

"It means that now is the time when the great and new thing will come into the world. But as yet no one knows what it will be."

Capella shouted across the sky to Aldebaran: "Look! I see three kings, coming from the east."

And Aldebaran shouted back: "Look! I see Herod trembling upon his throne."

Vega shouted below to Sirius: "Look! There are shepherds in the field keeping watch over their sheep, and they are made wondrously afraid of the star. They know now what it means."

And the Northern Star, around which the earth goes, cried aloud: "There is a new-born child in a Bethlehem manger; and harken, the angels are breaking into our midst with a great light and a singing of hallelujahs."

Each star asked of his neighbour star: "Is it the child that is born that we have been waiting for these thousand years? Has he come to fulfil our expectations?" And among themselves they whispered: "Let us ask Orion."

So they shouted across to the king of stars, and to the

earth below it sounded as if they were singing together, while Orion sang above the rest: "Truly it is the child new-born that is the great thing prophesied."

That was the Good Night. It is the only good night the world has ever known. That is why men keep it as they keep no other night in the year. Some time, in another thousand years or less, there may come another good night. Even now the stars may be waiting for it. Who knows?

5. Schnitzle, Schnotzle, and Schnootzle

FROM THE AUSTRIAN TIROL

Carol of the Cobblers

Bring the Christmas in—
Bring the Christmas in.
Tap and peg and sew the leather
Strong for winter's harshest weather.

Bring the Christmas in—
Bring the Christmas in.
Stop all work and light the candles;
Reverently put out His sandals.

Bring the Christmas in—
Bring the Christmas in.
Bring in the Child. While we are waiting
Purge us clean of sin and hating.

Bring the Christmas in—
Bring the Christmas in.
Hush, His steps, mayhap He's coming;
Make for Him a blithesome homing.

Bring the Christmas in—
Bring the Christmas in.
Carol clear, casting all fear out.
May His sandals wear the year out.
Bring the Christmas in—
Bring the Christmas in.

5. Schnitzle, Schnotzle, and Schnootzle

THE Tirol straddles the Alps and reaches one hand into Italy and another into Austria. There are more mountains in the Tirol than you can count and every Alp has its story.

Long ago, some say on the Brenner-Alp, some say on the Mitterwald-Alp, there lived the king of all the goblins of the Tirol, and his name was Laurin. King Laurin. His kingdom was under the earth, and all the gold and silver of the mountains he owned. He had a daughter, very young and very lovely, not at all like her father, who had a bulbous nose, big ears, and a squat figure, and looked as old as the mountains. She loved flowers and was sad that none grew inside her father's kingdom.

"I want a garden of roses—red roses, pink roses, blush roses, flame roses, shell roses, roses like the sunrise and the sunset." This she said one day to her father. And the king laughed and said she should have just such a garden. They would roof it with crystal, so that the sun would pour into the depths of the kingdom and make the roses grow lovely and fragrant. The garden was planted and every rare and exquisite rose bloomed in it. And so much colour they spread upwards on the mountains around that the snow caught it and the mortals living in the valley pointed at it with wonder. "What is it makes our Alps so rosy, so glowing?" they asked. And they spoke of it ever after as the alpen-glow.

I have told you this that you might know what kind of goblin King Laurin was. He was merry, and he liked to play pranks and have fun. He liked to go abroad into the valleys where the mortals lived, or pop into a herdsman's hut halfway up the mountain. There were men who said they had seen him—that small squat figure with a bulbous nose and big ears—gambolling with the goats on a summer day. And now I begin my story. It is an old one that Tirolese mothers like to tell their children.

Long ago there lived in one of the valleys a very poor cobbler indeed. His wife had died and left him with three children, little boys, all of them—Fritzl, Franzl, and Hansl. They lived in a hut so small there was only one room in it, and in that was the cobbler's bench, a hearth for cooking, a big bed full of straw, and on the wall racks for a few dishes, and, of course, there was a table with a settle and some stools. They needed few dishes or pans, for there was never much to cook or eat. Sometimes the cobbler would mend the Sunday shoes of a farmer, and then there was good goats' milk to drink. Sometimes he would mend the holiday shoes of the baker, and then there was the good long crusty loaf of bread to eat. And sometimes he mended the shoes of the butcher, and then there was the good stew, cooked with meat in the pot, and noodles, leeks, and herbs. When the cobbler gathered the little boys around the table and they had said their grace, he would laugh and clap his hands and sometimes even dance. "Ha-ha!" he would shout. "Today we have the good . . . what? Ah-h . . . today we eat . . . Schnitzle, Schnotzle, and Schnootzle!"

With that he would swing the kettle off the hook and fill every bowl brimming full, and Fritzl, Franzl, and Hansl would eat until they had had enough. Ach, those were the good days—the days of having Schnitzle, Schnotzle, and Schnootzle. Of course, the cobbler was making up nonsense and nothing else, but the stew tasted so much better because of the nonsense.

Now a year came, with every month following his brother on leaden feet. The little boys and the cobbler heard the month of March tramp out and April tramp in. They heard

June tramp out and July tramp in. And every month marched heavier than his brother. And that was because war was among them again. War, with workers taking up their guns and leaving mothers and children to care for themselves as best they could; and there was scant to pay even a poor cobbler for mending shoes. The whole village shuffled to church with the soles flapping and the heels lopsided, and the eyelets and buttons and straps quite gone.

Summer—that was not so bad. But winter came and covered up the good earth, and gone were the roots, the berries, the sorrel, and the corn. The tramp of November going out and December coming in was very loud indeed. The little boys were quite sure that the two months shook the hut as they passed each other on the mountainside.

As Christmas grew near, the little boys began to wonder if there would be any feast for them, if there would be the good father dancing about the room and laughing "Ha-ha," and singing "Ho-ho," and saying: "Now, this being Christmas Day we have the good . . . what?" And this time the little boys knew that they would never wait for their father to say it; they would shout themselves: "We know—it is the good Schnitzle, Schnotzle, and Schnootzle!" Ach, how very long it was since their father had mended shoes for the butcher! Surely—surely—there would be need soon again, with Christmas so near.

At last came the Eve of Christmas. The little boys climbed along the beginnings of the Brenner-Alp, looking for faggots. The trees had shed so little that year; every branch was green and grew fast to its tree, so few twigs had snapped, so little was there of dead, dried brush to fill their arms.

Their father came in when they had a small fire started, blowing his whiskers free of icicles, slapping his arms about his big body, trying to put warmth back into it. "Na-na, nobody will have a shoe mended today. I have asked everyone. Still there is good news. The soldiers are marching into the village. The inn is full. They will have boots that need mending, those soldiers. You will see." He pinched a cheek of each little boy; he winked at them and nodded his head. "You shall see—tonight I will come home with . . . what?"

"Schnitzle, Schnotzle, and Schnootzle," they shouted together, those three.

So happy they were they forgot there was nothing to eat for supper—not a crust, not a slice of cold porridge-pudding, not the smallest sup of goats' milk. "Will the soldiers have money to pay you?" asked Fritzl, the oldest.

"Not the soldiers, perhaps, but the captains. There might even be a general. I will mend the boots of the soldiers for nothing, for after all what day is coming tomorrow! They fight for us, those soldiers; we mend for them, ja? But a general—he will have plenty of money."

The boys stood about while their father put all his tools, all his pieces of leather into a rucksack; while he wound and wound and wound the woollen scarf about his neck, while he pulled the cap far down on his head. "It will be a night to freeze the ears off you," he said. "Now bolt the door after me, keep the fire burning with a little at a time; and climb into the straw-bed and pull the quilt over you. And let no one in!"

He was gone. They bolted the door; they put a little on the fire; they climbed into the big bed, putting Hansl, the smallest, in the middle. They pulled up the quilt, such a thin quilt to keep out so much cold! Straight and still and close together they lay, looking up at the little spot of light the fire made on the ceiling, watching their breath go upwards in icy spurts. With the going of the sun the wind rose. First it whispered: it whispered of good fires in big chimneys; it whispered of the pines on the mountainsides; it whispered of snow loosening and sliding over the glaciers. Then it began to blow: it blew hard, it blew quarrelsome, it blew cold and colder. And at last it roared. It roared its wintry breath through the cracks in the walls and under the door. And Fritzl, Franzl, and Hansl drew closer together and shivered.

"Whee . . . ooh . . . bang, bang! Whee . . . ooh . . . bang, bang!"

"Is it the wind or someone knocking?" asked Franzl.

"It is the wind," said Fritzl.

"Whee . . . ooh . . . knock, knock!"

"Is it the wind or someone knocking?" asked Hansl.

"It is the wind *and* someone knocking!" said Fritzl.

He rolled out of the bed and went to the window. It looked out directly on the path to the door. "Remember what our father said: do not open it," said Franzl.

But Fritzl looked and looked. Close to the hut, beaten against it by the wind, stood a little man no bigger than

Hansl. He was pounding on the door. Now they could hear him calling: "Let me in! I tell you, let me in!"

"Oh, don't, don't!" cried Hansl.

"I must," said Fritzl. "He looks very cold. The wind is tearing at him as a wolf tears at a young lamb"; and with that he drew the bolt and into the hut skipped the oddest little man they had ever seen. He had a great peaked cap tied onto his head with deer-thongs. He had a round red face out of which stuck a bulbous nose, like a fat plum on a pudding. He had big ears. And his teeth were chattering so hard they made the stools to dance. He shook his fist at the three little boys. "Ach, kept me waiting. Wanted to keep all the good food, all the good fire to yourselves? Na-na, that is no kind of hospitality."

He looked over at the little bit of a fire on the hearth, making hardly any heat in the hut. He looked at the empty table, not a bowl set or a spoon beside it. He took up the big pot, peered into it, turned it upside down to make sure nothing was clinging to the bottom, set it down with a bang. "So—you have already eaten it all. Greedy boys. But if you have saved no feast for me, you can at least warm me." With that he climbed into the big straw-bed with Franzl and Hansl, with his cap still tied under his chin. Fritzl tried to explain that they had not been greedy, that there had never been any food, not for days, to speak of. But he was too frightened of the little man, of his eyes as sharp and blue as ice, of his mouth so grumbling.

"Roll over, roll over," the little man was shouting at the

two in the bed. "Can't you see I have no room? Roll over and give me my half of the quilt."

Fritzl saw that he was pushing his brothers out of the bed. "Na-na," he said, trying to make peace with their guest. "They are little, those two. There is room for all if we but lie quiet." And he started to climb into the bed himself, pulling gently at the quilt that there might be a corner for him.

But the little man bounced and rolled about shouting: "Give me room, give me more quilt. Can't you see I'm cold? I call this poor hospitality to bring a stranger inside your door, give him nothing to eat, and then grudge him bed and covering to keep him warm." He dug his elbow into the side of skinny little Hansl.

"Ouch!" cried the boy.

Fritzl began to feel angry. "Sir," he said, "sir, I pray you to be gentle with my little brother. And I am sorry there has been nothing to give you. But our father, the cobbler, has gone to mend shoes for the soldiers. When he returns we look for food. Truly, this is a night to feast and to share. So if you will but lie still until he comes I can promise you . . ."

The little man rolled over and stuck his elbow into Fritzl's ribs. "Promise—promise. Na-na, what good is a promise? Come get out of bed and give me your place." He drew up his knees, put his feet in the middle of Fritzl's back and pushed with a great strength. The next moment the boy was spinning across the room. "There you go," roared the little man after him. "If you must keep warm turn cartwheels, turn them fast."

For a moment Fritzl stood sullenly by the small speck of fire. He felt bruised and very angry. He looked over at the bed. Sure enough, the greedy little man had rolled himself up in the quilt leaving only a short corner of it for the two younger boys. He had taken more than half of the straw for himself, and was even then pushing and digging at Hansl. He saw Franzl raise himself up and take the place of his littlest brother, that he should get the digs.

Brrr . . . it was cold! Before he knew it Fritzl was doing as he had been told, turning cartwheels around the room. He had rounded the table and was coming toward the bed when —plop! Plop—plop—plop! Things were falling out of his pockets every time his feet swung high over his head. Plop—plop—plop! The two younger boys were sitting up in bed. It was their cries of astonishment which brought Fritzl's feet back to the floor again, to stay. In a circle about the room, he had left behind him a golden trail of oranges. Such oranges—big as two fists! And sprinkled everywhere between were comfits wrapped in gold and silver paper. Fritzl stood and gaped at them.

"Here, you, get out and keep warm yourself!" shouted the little man as he dug Franzl in the ribs. "Cartwheels for you, boy!" And the next minute Franzl was whirling in cartwheels about the room. Plop—plop—plop—things were dropping out of his pockets: Christmas buns, Christmas cakes covered with icing, with plums, with anise and caraway seeds.

The little man was digging Hansl now in the ribs. "Lazy boy, greedy boy. Think you can have the bed to yourself now? Na-na, I'll have it! Out you go!" And he put his feet against the littlest boy's back and pushed him onto the floor. "Cartwheels . . ." he began; but Fritzl, forgetting his amazement at what was happening, shouted: "But, sir, he is too little. He cannot turn . . ."

"Hold him up in the corner, then. You keep warmer when your heels are higher than your head. Step lively there. Take a leg, each of you, and be quick about it."

So angry did the little man seem, so fiery and determined, that Fritzl and Franzl hurried their little brother over to the chimney corner, stood him on his head and each held a leg. Donner and Blitzen! What happened then! Whack—whack—whickety-whack! Whack—whack—whickety-whack! Pelting the floor like hail against the roof came silver and gold pieces, all pouring out of Hansl's pockets.

Fritzl began to shout, Franzl began to dance. Hansl began to shout: "Let me down, let me down!" When they did the three little boys danced around the pile, taking hands, singing "Tra-la-la," and "Fiddle-de-dee," and "Ting-a-ling-a-ling," until their breath was gone and they could dance no longer. They looked over at the bed and Fritzl was opening his mouth to say: "Now, if you please, sir, we can offer you some Christmas cheer . . ." But the bed was empty, the quilt lay in a heap on the floor. The little man had gone.

The three little boys were gathering up the things on the floor—putting oranges into the big wooden bowl, buns and cakes on to the two platters, silver and gold pieces into this dish and that. And right in the midst of it in came their father, stamping, puffing in through the door. He had brought bread, he had brought milk, he had brought meat for the good stew—and noodles.

Such a wonder, such a clapping of hands, such a singing as they worked to get ready the Christmas feast! Fritzl began the story about their Christmas guest; Franzl told it mid-through; but little Hansl finished, making his brothers stand him in the corner again on his head to show just how it was that all the silver and gold had tumbled out of his pockets.

"Na-na," said the cobbler, "we are the lucky ones. I did not know it was true; always I thought it was a tale the grandfathers told the children. The saying goes that King Laurin comes every year at the Christmas to one hut—one family—to play his tricks and share his treasure horde."

"He was a very ugly little man," said Hansl. "He dug us in our ribs and took all the bed for himself."

"That was the king—that is the way he plays at being fierce. Say: '*Komm, Herr Jesus, und sei unser Gast,*' then draw up the stools. Ah-h . . . what have we to eat?"

The little boys shouted the answer all together: "Schnitzle—Schnotzle—and Schnootzle!"

6. The Gold of Bernardino

AN ANCIENT LEGEND OF CANTABRIA

A Carol from the North of Spain

Sing,
dance,
whisper along the way.
What shall we whisper?
It is Christ's Day.

Sing,
dance,
what shall we bring?
Let no hand go empty
of gifts for the King.

Sing,
dance,
a cake baked brown and sweet
Rosita brings
for Him to eat.

Sing,
dance,
Miguel brings a mouse,
grey and small,
for Christ's house.

Sing,
dance,
whisper along the way.
What shall we whisper?
It is Christ's Day.

6. The Gold of Bernardino

CENTURIES before the Armada sailed from the bay of Vigo to make war on English ships, there lived high up in the Cantabrian Hills a peasant. He was a strong giant of a man, with gentle hands for creatures and children, a quiet, friendly way of speaking, and an exceedingly simple heart. He lived by himself with the oxen that drew his plough, the goats that gave him milk, and the dog, small and black, that ran bouncingly at his heels.

No churches had yet been built in Spain. But there came one spring a saintly man, a friar, climbing the hills to the peasant's hut, there to dwell with him many days while he told of a new God and of His Son, a holier man than all other men, one who had been born and had died and been born again. Every night, after the day's ploughing, the friar would read out of a small handwritten book about this Son of God, this Jesus the Christ. He had much to tell: a new religion had been called after Him—Christianity; and there were many stories not written down which had been passed from mouth to mouth.

"I would become a Christian," said the peasant. "I would follow this Jesus the Christ."

It came naturally therefore that the friar before he left should baptize the peasant. He gave him the name of Bernardino, by which he became known throughout Cantabria. Now, being one who seldom had intercourse with other men, Bernardino was fearful lest he forget all the friar had told him; so he began repeating to the beasts the stories and all that had been read out of the handwritten book concerning the sayings of Jesus the Christ. While the peasant cleared new land and ploughed, he would talk with the oxen, saying: "Slow and gentle ones, it is well that you should hear. Listen then: 'And that same day went Jesus out of the house and sat by the sea. . . .' "

When he milked the goats at nightfall he would time his words to the dripping in his firkin: "Good my brothers, this is for thy ears, these blessings: 'Blessed are the poor in spirit——' "

And before he slept, with the dog lying beside the hearth, he would tell of the lame, the halt, and the blind, and how they were healed by the laying-on of hands: "Small, faithful one, He was of all men the most holy."

He fitted the story of Jesus the Christ to the seasons, so that with the winter solstice he began with the shepherds, of their watching, of the angels, the star, the manger, and the new-born Babe. " 'Hosanna! Glory to God in the highest!' That is good; but hearken to something better, my beasts: 'On Earth peace, good will toward men!' That is something for beasts and men to carry in their hearts always."

He would tell with wonder, with bitterness, with grief that made his eyes to overflow and sent tears coursing down the furrows of his cheeks only to fall upon the furrows of the earth, all that had to do with the life and death of Jesus the Christ. But always he came back to the winter solstice with a fresh heart, always he began: "Listen, lowly ones, we come again to the birth." Then only did he know joy unbound.

From that first telling of the birth had sprung a great resolve, and this he shared with no man, only the beasts: "I shall go someday to Bethlehem at Christmas-time, when again the Child is born. I, too, shall worship at His manger. You shall see!"

It meant gold for passage, gold for food, and a gift when he should reach the lowly stable. Ships of many countries, from the east, the south, the north, were always making port at the harbour, needing to be revictualled. He would carry half of his harvest each year to the sea and sell it for gold. He would talk with sailors about this place called Bethlehem, in Judea. He would find out from them the length of time for the pilgrimage and the cost.

From the time he made that first journey to the harbour, Bernardino strung a leather pouch about his loins and in it he put his first piece of gold. It would take ten pieces for his undertaking, and a half-year's time. If he started after the autumn equinox he would be back in time for the spring planting. That was good! The beasts would care for themselves; he would have much to tell them when he returned.

Bernardino was a young man when the friar had baptized him; he was at his prime when the pouch was full and the autumn equinox at hand. The gold from this last harvest would provide the gift for the Child. He never doubted he would find Bethlehem, never doubted that the Child would be there, new-born.

His eve of departure came. The clumsy two-wheeled cart was loaded against the morning's journey. Bernardino was stooping over the hearth, putting into the carefully raked embers the oaten-cakes, wrapped in cabbage leaves, which would furnish some of the food he would need. He chanced to look up. A small, struggling figure was weaving its uncertain way up the path to the hut. Before the peasant could regain his feet the figure had stumbled forward and dropped face down not two metres from the door.

Bernardino reached the figure and crouched beside it. It was a lad, his clothes torn from him, his back lashed in places clean to the bone. "Who has dared?" The peasant was angered at what he saw—a lad so small, so young, to be so trod upon. He lifted him with great tenderness, bore him inside, and put him carefully down upon his bed of skins. Then he gathered healing herbs and gum from the trees, making of these a balm to put upon the wounds. Coming to consciousness, the lad would have fled had he not been so weak from loss of blood. It took no strength to restrain him; but it took much gentling of speech, much coaxing, to get him to swallow the warm milk Bernardino held to his lips. Stark terror was in the lad's eyes. "That, too, will take healing," Bernardino thought.

A day came when the lad was well enough to run about. Twice now his lips had broken into a smile when Bernardino had clapped his hands at the lad's quick understanding of a tongue strange to him. The moon had waxed from first quarter to full when a man climbed the hill; he was laced into a leather cuirass and carried a sword. The lad took flight at sight of him, and by signs the stranger made Bernardino know he had come hunting the lad, a slave, to take him back to his ship from which he had fled. In the end the peasant brought out his gold and paid the ten pieces demanded for the lad's freedom.

"It is well," the peasant thought. "Now I will have someone to leave with land and beasts when I go." And he bent his whole strength and heart to teaching the boy to forget fear and understand what freedom meant, and in helping him to a mastery of his tongue—this that he might have human ears in which to pour the stories of Jesus the Christ and all that had been written down in the small book.

Harvests multiplied. Now in the autumn when he and the lad went together to the harbour to sell the grain, the cabbages, the goats' cheese, and sour wine, there were two gold pieces to put into the leather pouch that hung about the peasant's loins. Five years beat themselves out as swiftly as a swallow beats his way across the water, and again came the time for Bernardino's departure. His mind and heart were filled with the joy of going, of forecasting that moment when his feet would cross the threshold of the stable and he would be kneeling there before the Child. "It will all be to tell to you when I come back. Watch for the star. Always I look for it, for who can tell when again it may appear and mark the way."

Night had fallen. The oaten-cakes were done and the lad sat, peeling off the burned cabbage leaves, and laying each cake carefully in the sack Bernardino would carry with him. Suddenly the quiet of the night was cut in twain by a shouting of voices, and out of the darkness came four robed figures —friars, holy men, even such as had once come hither years before. Bernardino rose to welcome them, to give them food and bed them down as best he could, he and the lad going out to the shed to sleep with the beasts. But before he went the friars had a strange thing to tell. All over God's world men were beginning to build churches in which to worship Jesus the Christ. Such a church they had come to build, and a monastery to house their holy order. They would need the help of strong men; they would need all the gold the followers of Jesus the Christ could bring together.

To this strange tale there was but one answer for Bernardino. He must give his gold. Would he ever have heard of the Child, or Bethlehem, had not a holy man brought the tale to him? He would stay and help build this church. It might be the will of the new God that he do his worshipping here, and not in Bethlehem.

So began a new life for Bernardino the peasant. He worked the ground as little as was needful to feed himself, the lad, and the four who had come. From the first coming of light back of the hills to the last shaft of it beyond the sea, he worked at the felling of trees, the shaping of great beams, the curving of them to a vaulted roof. As they worked together the holy men taught Bernardino certain salvés and glorias and chants that had come to be part of the worship. These they sang and the hills gave them back in full echo.

It took years for the building of church and monastery. When all was completed Bernardino had become an old man, having more years than he could remember. There had been times when rebellion and anger filled his heart, when he fought against the work allotted him, and the dying, piece by piece, of his dream of Bethlehem. But these times grew less fearful, less often, and he found much consolation in the worship and prayer in the chapel. There had come from some far distant place a figure of Jesus the Christ upon the cross, with thorns to crown Him, and another of Mary His Mother in a blue robe and a golden crown on her head. The brothers called her the Virgin of Light, and Bernardino found much solace in kneeling at matin and complin, telling her all that was in his heart. It was hard to pray to the One upon the cross, for never had he so conceived Him. Often he protested this to the brothers: "Why hang Him there, year after year? Preach the Crucifixion, yes; and the Resurrection at Easter. But show Jesus the Christ as the Child new-born—always new-born. That is what we must remember. It is the birth we worship, not the death."

The older he grew the oftener he protested: "It is Bethlehem we seek—not Calvary. Come, let us have here the Child, lying within its manger."

But who had ever heard of such a thing put into a consecrated church, built upon ground made holy? "He is getting more ancient than the oldest tree," said one. "Sometimes I think he must have come to Spain with the good Santiago," said another. "He is growing foolish as old men will," said a third. "He will soon die."

But Bernardino did not die. He lived on, far beyond his allotted years. Many friars had come to the monastery; pilgrims climbed the hills to worship there. The brothers gave Bernardino light tasks to perform that would not try his waning strength. But as he drew water, brought faggots from the woods, out of a mind often befogged would come to him that wonder of why he should live on. Why had he not died as those first friars with whom he had worked to build the church? And one day the answer to this came. How could he die until he had seen Bethlehem? Had he not made that promise to worship where the living Christ was born? It was not enough to kneel before a dying Christ; he must find the living One.

There came a winter of great snows and high piercing winds that shook the monastery on the hills and chilled the brothers to their marrow. Bernardino was let bring his goatskins inside and sleep beside the fire in the hall. So it happened that on the Eve of Christmas, when the brothers had withdrawn after complin to their cells to await the celebration of the Christmas Mass, Bernardino lay asleep. And as he slept he dreamed:

Youth had come back to him—strength to his limbs and joy to his heart. He felt again the impending journey to Bethlehem, and raising himself to an elbow he looked upon the hearth to see if the oaten-cakes were cooking there. But the hearth was empty. He felt for the pouch about his loins; no longer did it hang there to hold his gold. Where was it? Where had the gold gone? The winter solstice was at hand; he must hurry to reach Bethlehem in time for the birth.

Of its own accord the doorway of the monastery opened and in there came oxen and goats and a dog, small and black. The noises they made were those of beasts to a loving master. They came, rubbing heads against his limbs, while the dog licked eagerly at his hand and whined. "Good!" said Bernardino, "we go together." Holding fast by the oxen's horns he raised himself, and putting his arms over their necks he walked with them, not to the door, not outside to the winter's night, but across the hall, along the cloisters, to the chapel door.

It did not seem strange that they should enter the church together. Enter and kneel. Nor did it seem strange that where the altar had been there was a manger. The light from tapering candles filled the rude stall to overflowing. It shone upon Mary's face, she kneeling as they knelt. It shone upon the angels' choir, their wings interlaced, their hands raised in salutation. But far more radiant than these it shone upon the face of the Child, lying quietly upon His straw.

"See—we are come, little Holy One. Or is it that Thou hast come to us? What matters it? It is the night of the birth—we are here at last to worship." Very tenderly Bernardino held out the forefinger of his right hand and worked it slowly within the small closed fist of the Child. He felt it tighten, a strong tight-holding grip. The Child's eyes opened and there was in them the look of one long-known, long-loved.

But others who had come to worship had brought gifts. Again Bernardino felt for the pouch and found it gone. Then did he look up, wondering, perplexed, and saw an angel's hand extended, and holding a leather pouch. "It is thine, take it. We have but kept it for thee."

When the brothers gathered in the hall, there to form the processional for early Mass, they found the hearth deserted.

Gaining the chapel they looked with consternation upon the ancient figure kneeling there, the creatures about him. The Father Superior paused to waken him; and then he saw, as did all the brotherhood, at what lowly place the peasant was worshipping: a manger, although to them no manger was visible; the Child, for only upon a child did the human soul so pour forth such love and adoration. They could have sworn on Holy Writ that, clasped within the ancient wrinkled hand, there lay that of a young child. What they did see was the pouch beside him.

"The gold," they whispered one to another. "It was in such a leather pouch he brought his offering for the church, so the records say." Ten pieces of gold it held when they counted it. "Look, here are now the same ten pieces within."

As the spring drew near, the brothers talked often of Bernardino's going, the time and manner of it.

"He was a good man—none better ever walked the earth."

"He consecrated his life as a true follower of Jesus the Christ. We, ourselves, have done no more."

"That strange idea he had about the manger, the coming to worship there, before all other places!"

It was not strange that out of talk such as this should have come the wish to honour Bernardino's memory. "Of all things he would have liked best," said the Father Superior, "what say you?"

And so it came to pass that throughout the full green of spring, the sweet lagging of summer, the glowing and plenty of garnered harvest, those brothers who could carve bent all their skill and time upon the making of a manger and figures to kneel about it. When the next Christmas Eve came, the manger was placed full lovingly upon the steps of the altar. There were Mary and Joseph, angels in attendance. And kneeling among the shepherds the brothers had made the figure of Bernardino holding out his offering of gold to the Child.

That was the first Nativity put into a Spanish church. That was the first Christmas Mass sung to the Child. It has made this birth everlasting. And in the kneeling figure of Bernardino has come down the memory of a great and simple man.

7. The Wishing Well

FROM THE OLD FRENCH PROVINCE OF LANGUEDOC

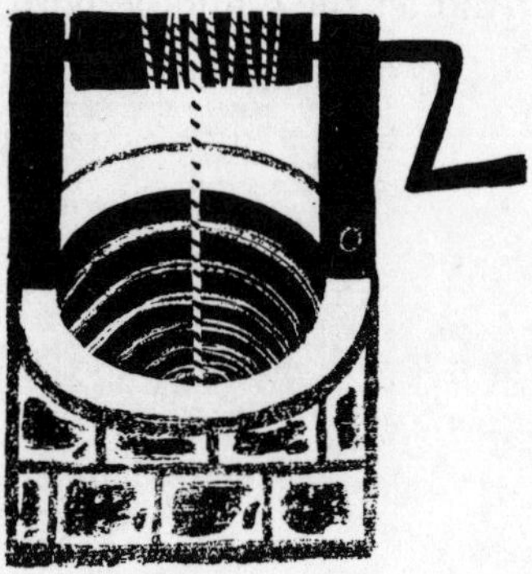

An Old French Carol

He comes, His throne the manger;
He comes, His shrine the stall.
The ox, the ass, the servants
Of Him who made us all.
The House of Bread His birthplace
The Prince of wine and corn;
Lift up your gates, ye Princes,
And let the Child be born.

7. The Wishing Well

IN the ancient province of Languedoc there is a wishing well. It lies on the road which runs from Nîmes to the Mediterranean, and every Christmas Eve come young, come old, to wish for themselves good fortune and abundance. Or, if life has gone ill with them, to wish themselves free of their troubles. Like all wishing wells, it is a holy well, blessed long ago by Mary the Mother of Jesus.

Here is a legend that French mothers tell to their children:

In the days of Louis the Grand Monarch, there lived two

farmers about a kilometre's distance from the well, one on this side of the road and one on the other. Their barnyards faced each other, as barnyards will, and when the cock in one barnyard crowed: "Co-co-ri-co," the cock in the other barnyard answered him.

Now the farmer on this side of the road owned a white goose—so plump, so sleek of feather, so snowy-white—the very perfection of a goose. While the farmer on the other side of the road owned a grey ass, alert of ears, agile of hoof, gallant and charming in all ways common to asses.

Every day the goose wandered close to the hedge searching for beetles. Every day she cast shy, amorous glances at the ass grazing close behind his hedge. Soon the ass learned the art of grazing with one eye turned aloft, that he might follow the trail of the white goose. "On my word," said the ass, "never have I seen such a goose. She is a very queen among geese. Why am I but an ass and the road between us?"

Before too long the goose caught the admiring cock of the ass's eye, and she sighed sorrowfully: "Ah, me! What a splendid creature. Never have I seen such nobility, such elegance, such charm of manner. Why am I but a goose?"

As time went on, they were not content merely to exchange glances. The ass was consumed with his desire to tell the goose of his love. The goose yearned to tell of her admiration for the ass. One day the ass could contain himself no longer. He lifted up his head and brayed, long, loud. It was like the very blast of a trumpet.

The goose was transfixed. "What a voice! What magnitude of sound! He proclaims himself like a champion. Ah, me, if I could but know what he is saying!" And in a great despair she opened her bill and hissed.

The ass heard. He was enchanted, but he was likewise in despair. "What sibilant tones! What gentle, soothing sounds! Mayhap my Lady Goose is telling me of her love, sighing for me, and I shall never know. Alas—alas—to be an ass and have so little understanding!"

Spring saw the beginning of their love; summer saw it ripen. When autumn fell, so completely taken up were they with their sighings, their hissing and braying, that both barnyards were on the point of a revolt. "A terrible state of affairs," said a duck in one barnyard to the oldest hen. "I can no longer make my ducklings behave. They refuse to listen to me, so taken up they are with watching the goings-on of our white goose with that grey ass across the way."

"Such an example to young birds," said the hen. "No one pays any attention to me any longer when I cackle the addition of an egg to the poultry house. Pretty goings-on, I call it, for a goose to be setting her cap for an ass."

On the other side of the road a grey gander was saying to the first cock: "Dear, dear, I don't know what to do! Good friend, I wish you would speak to that ass. My geese have grown so jealous of the goose across the road I can do nothing with them. They are impertinent. They answer back. They have their necks nearly craned off watching that silly bird. I tell you, my temper is gone. I implore you—say something."

But for once the cock was humble. His head twitched nervously in the direction of the ass. "My good fellow, the truth is I haven't the courage. I have seen what that ass can do with his heels too often to dare risk his displeasure. He would resent it, you know, from one of us. He feels superior. The thing to do is to shut our eyes to the whole affair. It can't last. Something is bound to happen."

The cock was right—something did happen. Winter came, and with it the season of Noel. Early on the Eve of Christmas two lovers passed along the road between the barnyards. They loitered, as lovers will, and because the moments spent together were few and therefore very precious, "If we could but marry," they sighed. "Ah, if we could see happiness together—one little cottage—a small farm—a few geese——"

Now the goose was at her accustomed place, close to the hedge. And the ass was at his. So they heard all. And while it is not possible for a creature to understand what a bird talks about, nor for a bird to understand a creature, it is given to both to understand the speech of humans. The goose sighed with the lovers. "Poor things, they are separated even as the ass and myself by some great trouble." And she stood very still to hear more.

"It is the fault of our mothers," said the maid, "especially of your mother. If your mother were only young, if she had no scolding tongue—then some good man would be glad enough to marry her. Then we could marry and have the farm."

"It is not my mother, it is yours. If she were cured of all her ailments then she could spare you from minding the house and the children." The youth said it sullenly.

"Let us not quarrel, beloved. There is the wishing well." And the maid drew her arm tenderly within his.

"You believe?"

"In the well? To be sure. Only last year Neighbour Gicot wished that his cow might have two calves in the spring. And behold—she had them!"

"We lose nothing by going. Let us make haste. You shall wish for a cure of all your mother's ailments. I will wish for a husband for my mother. Come!"

Holding to each other they passed down the road, and the ass brayed after them: "Alas, alas! Human beings are no more fortunate than creatures where love is concerned."

Until darkness fell, the ass from his barnyard, the goose from hers, watched the never-ceasing procession of humans on their way to the Wishing Well. The ass understood their pilgrimage, for had he not taken grain to the mill to be ground season after season? And did not the mill stand near to the wishing well? But the goose understood nothing. "What is all this talk of wishing and well?" she asked herself many times. At last, driven by curiosity, she went in search of the cock.

She found him asleep on his perch and woke him, demanding: "Tell me—why are there so many abroad on the road tonight?"

The cock would have been very angry had it not pleased his vanity to be questioned. "It concerns the night, first. This is the Eve of Noel, a holy night. Then it has to do with the wishing well. Whoever drinks of it upon this night and makes a wish—that wish shall be granted."

"And do you believe that?" asked the goose.

"What I believe or you believe does not matter. The humans believe and it works for them." He ruffled his feathers and settled himself for sleep.

For a long time the goose pondered what she had heard; it was long past bedtime for all the barnyard. A respectable goose should retire. But to the contrary, the white goose moved slowly along the hedge, feeling with her bill for a worn place in it. Here she started to dig, scooping out dirt, making a hollow by which she could work her way under the hedge to the road beyond.

At last she was free. Gaining the road she followed along its edge, the way of other pilgrims. Down the long way she waddled—this side, that side. She came to the wishing well and hid herself behind some bushes to watch how humans made their wishes on this night.

There was a sailor who wished for good voyages. There was a merchant who wished for good cargoes. There was a farmer who wished for fat crops. There was a lover who sighed and wished that he might gain the heart of his lady-love. There was an ancient one who wished himself free of his malady; and there was a young maid who wished for a dowry. And each knelt making his wish, cupped his hand in the well, sipped, and made the sign of the cross over the well.

All this the goose noted well. And when the last human had departed she waddled to the brink, scooped water in her bill, waggled it down and across, and hissed feebly and with a sinking heart: "If it please you, Holy Mother, I wish to be a small grey ass!"

In the name of the Good God, what happened then! Such a changing—such a swelling—such a hardening here and softening there. The wish had hardly left her bill when it began to soften, to swell. Up from her head shot two towering ears. What legs she had stretched and stretched, and down from behind shot two more. Four legs she had now, with hoofs at the ends. And behind that a tail! It was unbelievable, it was unmanageable! And all her soft white feathers had become grey hair. "Ah, me"—and the sigh that came from her hairy lips was no longer sibilant—"one suffers much for love!" Feeling very foolish she lifted two of her four legs and put hoofs to ground, then two more. And so—moving clumsily along the road, she came at last to her barnyard.

And what of the grey ass? He waited and pondered. He changed his mind many times. He would and he wouldn't. But with a silent, empty road running away from him he gathered for a spring, cleared the hedge, and was down the road at last, his hoofs striking hard against the road. The wishing well was deserted, but he knew from long gossip what one did to get one's wish. He knelt at the brink, thrust his muzzle into the water, nodded his sign of the cross, and brayed softly: "Holy Mother, if it please you, make me a fine white gander!"

Name of names! What a shrinking! What a vanishing! Away like thin grey smoke went his proud ears; away went his most necessary tail. His fine grey coat became white-washed in the wink of an eye. His soft, nibbling muzzle was gone and in its place were two small board-like protuberances out of which came a hissing sound. Mary, Joseph, and Jesus! What had happened to him? He steadied himself upon his two short legs. Swaying from side to side like a sailor just off his ship, he waddled slowly back to his barnyard, hissing all the way: "This love, now, this love! What does it do to one? Where does it lead one? Is there an ending to it?"

The sun was well up on Christmas Morning when both farmers looked out upon their barnyards; and the farmer on this side of the road exclaimed: "Can it be possible—my neighbour's grey ass is in my barnyard?" And he hurried forth to return the creature.

At the same moment the farmer on the other side looked out and exclaimed: "Can I believe my eyes—my neighbour's white goose is in my barnyard?" And he hurried out to return it.

So it happened that both farmers met in the middle of the

road to make their exchanges. And while they wished each other a *Joyeux Noël*, and asked after the health of their families, the white gander who had been a grey ass and the grey ass who had been a white goose gazed in despair at each other. Suddenly the ass opened her muzzle and brayed, loud and long: "What an ass am I!"

And the white gander, understanding nothing but catching the sound of sorrow in that braying, opened his bill and hissed: "Alas, alas, what a goose I am!"

And from that day to this, when a grey ass meets a white goose, that is what they say to each other.

8. The Voyage of the Wee Red Cap

A CHRISTMAS FAIRYTALE

The Song of Saint Stephen

8. The Voyage of the Wee Red Cap

IT was the Eve of Saint Stephen, and Teig sat alone by his fire with naught in his cupboard but a pinch of tea and a bare mixture of meal, and a heart inside of him as soft and warm as the ice on the water-bucket outside the door. The turf was near burnt on the hearth—a handful of golden cinders left, just; and Teig took to counting them greedily on his fingers.

Acknowledgment is hereby made to Harper & Brothers for permission to use "The Voyage of the Wee Red Cap" from *This Way to Christmas* by Ruth Sawyer.

"There's one, two, three, an' four an' five," he laughed. "Faith, there be more bits o' real gold hid undther the loose clay in the corner."

It was the truth; and it was the scraping and scrooching for the last piece that had left Teig's cupboard bare of a Christmas dinner.

"Gold is betther nor eatin' an' dthrinkin'. An' if ye have naught to give, there'll be naught asked of ye." And he laughed again.

He was thinking of the neighbours, and the doles of food and piggins of milk that would pass over their thresholds that night to the vagabonds and paupers who were sure to come begging. And on the heels of that thought followed another: Who would be giving old Barney his dinner? Barney lived a stone's throw from Teig, alone in a wee tumbled-in cabin; and for a score of years past Teig had stood on the doorstep every Christmas Eve and, making a hollow of his two hands, had called across the road:

"Hey, there, Barney, will ye come over for a sup?"

And Barney had reached for his crutches—there being but one leg to him—and had come.

"Faith," said Teig, trying another laugh, "Barney can fast for the once; 'twill be all the same in a month's time." And he fell to thinking of the gold again.

A knock came at the door. Teig pulled himself down in his chair where the shadow would cover him, and held his tongue.

"Teig, Teig!" It was the Widow O'Donnelly's voice. "If ye are there, open your door. I have not got the pay for the spriggin' this month, an' the childher are needin' food."

But Teig put the leash on his tongue, and never stirred till he heard the tramp of her feet going on to the next cabin. Then he saw to it that the door was tight barred. Another knock came, and it was a stranger's voice this time:

"The other cabins are filled; not one but has its hearth crowded; will ye take us in—the two of us? The wind bites mortal sharp, not a morsel o' food have we tasted this day. Masther, will ye take us in?"

But Teig sat on, a-holding his tongue; and the tramp of the strangers' feet passed down the road. Others took their place—small feet, running. It was the miller's wee Cassie, and she called out as she ran by:

"Old Barney's watchin' for ye. Ye'll not be forgettin' him, will ye, Teig?"

And then the child broke into a song, sweet and clear, as she passed down the road:

Hearken all ye, 'tis the Feast o' Saint Stephen,
Mind that ye keep it this holy even.
Open your door an' greet ye the stranger,
For ye mind that the wee Lord had naught but a manger.
Mhuire as traugh!

Feed ye the hungry an' rest ye the weary,
This ye must do for the sake of Our Mary.

'Tis well that ye mind—ye who sit by the fire—
That the Lord He was born in a dark and cold byre.
Mhuire as traugh!

Teig put his fingers deep in his ears. "A million murdthering curses on them that won't let me be! Can't a man try to keep what is his without bein' pesthered by them that has only idled and wasted their days?"

And then the strange thing happened: hundreds and hundreds of wee lights began dancing outside the window, making the room bright; the hands of the clock began chasing each other round the dial; and the bolt of the door drew itself out. Slowly, without a creak or a cringe, the door opened, and in there trooped a crowd of the Good People. Their wee green cloaks were folded close about them, and each carried a rush candle.

Teig was filled with a great wonderment, entirely, when he saw the fairies, but when they saw him they laughed.

"We are takin' the loan o' your cabin this night, Teig," said they. "Ye are the only man hereabouts with an empty hearth an' we're needin' one."

Without saying more, they bustled about the room making ready. They lengthened out the table and spread and set it; more of the Good People trooped in bringing stools and food and drink. The pipers came last, and they sat themselves around the chimney-piece a-blowing their chanters and trying the drones. The feasting began and the pipers played, and never had Teig seen such a sight in his life. Suddenly, a wee man sang out:

"Clip clap, clip clap, I wish I had my wee red cap!" And out of the air there tumbled the neatest cap Teig ever laid his two eyes on. The wee man clapped it on his head, crying:

"I wish I was in Spain!" and—whist—up the chimney he went, and away out of sight.

It happened just as I am telling it. Another wee man called for his cap, and away he went after the first. And then another and another, until the room was empty and Teig sat alone again.

"By my soul," said Teig, "I'd like to travel that way myself! It's a grand savin' of tickets an' baggage; an' ye get to a place before ye've had time to change your mind. Faith, there's no harm done if I thry it."

So he sang the fairies' rhyme, and out of the air dropped a wee cap for him. For a moment the wonder had him, but the next he was clapping the hat on his head and crying:

"Spain!"

Then—whist—up the chimney he went after the fairies, and before he had time to let out his breath he was standing in the middle of Spain, and strangeness all about him.

He was in a great city. The doorways of the houses were hung with flowers and the air was warm and sweet with the smell of them. Torches burned along the streets, sweetmeat-sellers went about crying their wares, and on the steps of the cathedral crouched a crowd of beggars.

"What's the meanin' o' that?" asked Teig of one of the fairies.

"They are waiting for those that are hearing the Mass. When they come out, they give half of what they have to those that have nothing, so on this night of all the year there shall be no hunger and no cold."

And then far down the street came the sound of a child's voice, singing:

> Hearken all ye, 'tis the Feast o' Saint Stephen,
> Mind that ye keep it this holy even.

"Curse it!" said Teig. "Can a song fly afther ye?" And then he heard the fairies cry "Holland!" and cried "Holland!" too.

In one leap he was over France, and another over Belgium, and with the third he was standing by long ditches of frozen water, and over them glided hundreds upon hundreds of lads and maids. Outside each door stood a wee wooden shoe, empty. Teig saw scores of them as he looked down the ditch of a street.

"What is the meanin' o' those shoes?" he asked the fairies.

"Ye poor lad!" answered the wee man next to him. "Are ye not knowing anything? This is the Gift Night of the year, when every man gives to his neighbour."

A child came to the window of one of the houses, and in her hand was a lighted candle. She was singing as she put the light down close to the glass, and Teig caught the words:

Open your door an' greet ye the stranger,

For ye mind that the wee Lord had naught but a manger.
Mhuire as traugh!

" 'Tis the devil's work!" cried Teig, and he set the red cap more firmly on his head. "I'm for another country."

I cannot be telling you a half of the adventures Teig had that night, nor half the sights he saw. But he passed by fields that held sheaves of grain for the birds and doorsteps that held bowls of porridge for the wee creatures. He saw lighted trees, sparkling and heavy with gifts; and he stood outside the churches and watched the crowds pass in, bearing gifts to the Holy Mother and Child.

At last the fairies straightened their caps and cried: "Now for the great hall in the King of England's palace!"

Whist—and away they went, and Teig after them; and the first thing he knew he was in London, not an arm's length from the King's throne. It was a grander sight than he had seen in any other country. The hall was filled entirely with lords and ladies; and the great doors were open for the poor and the homeless to come in and warm themselves by the King's fire and feast from the King's table. And many a hungry soul did the King serve with his own hands.

Those that had anything to give gave it in return. It might be a bit of music played on a harp or a pipe, or it might be a dance or a song; but more often it was a wish, just, for good luck and safekeeping.

Teig was so taken up with the watching that he never

heard the fairies when they wished themselves off; moreover, he never saw the wee girl that was fed and went laughing away. But he heard a bit of her song as she passed through the door:

> Feed ye the hungry an' rest ye the weary,
> This ye must do for the sake of Our Mary.

Then the anger had Teig. "I'll stop your pestherin' tongue, once an' for all time!" and, catching the cap from his head, he threw it after her.

No sooner was the cap gone than every soul in the hall saw him. The next moment they were about him, catching at his coat and crying:

"Where is he from, what does he here? Bring him before the King!" And Teig was dragged along by a hundred hands to the throne where the King sat.

"He was stealing food," cried one.

"He was robbing the King's jewels," cried another.

"He looks evil," cried a third. "Kill him!"

And in a moment all the voices took it up and the hall rang with: "Aye, kill him, kill him!"

Teig's legs took to trembling, and fear put the leash on his tongue; but after a long silence he managed to whisper:

"I have done evil to no one—no one!"

"Maybe," said the King; "but have ye done good? Come, tell us, have ye given aught to anyone this night? If ye have, we will pardon ye."

Not a word could Teig say. Fear tightened the leash, for he was knowing full well there was no good to him that night.

"Then ye must die," said the King. "Will ye try hanging or beheading?"

"Hanging, please, your Majesty," said Teig.

The guards came rushing up and carried him off. But as he was crossing the threshold of the hall a thought sprang at him and held him, just.

"Your Majesty," he called after him, "will ye grant me a last request?"

"I will," said the King.

"Thank ye. There's a wee red cap that I'm mortal fond of, and I lost it a while ago; if I could be hung with it on, I would hang a deal more comfortable."

The cap was found and brought to Teig.

"Clip clap, clip clap, for my wee red cap, I wish I was home," he sang.

Up and over the heads of the dumfounded guard he flew—whist, and away out of sight. When he opened his eyes again, he was sitting close by his own hearth, with the fire burnt low. The hands of the clock were still, the bolt was fixed firm in the door. The fairies' lights were gone, and the only bright thing was the candle burning in old Barney's cabin across the road.

A running of feet sounded outside, and then a snatch of a song:

'Tis well that ye mind—ye who sit by the fire—
That the Lord He was born in a dark and cold byre.
Mhuire as traugh!

"Wait ye, whoever ye are!" And Teig was away to the corner, digging fast at the loose clay, as a terrier digs at a bone. He filled his hands full of the shining gold, then hurried to the door, unbarring it.

The miller's wee Cassie stood there, peering at him out of the darkness.

"Take those to the Widow O'Donnelly, do ye hear? And take the rest to the store. Ye tell Jamie to bring up all that he has that is eatable an' dthrinkable; and to the neighbours ye say: 'Teig's keepin' the feast this night.' Hurry, away!"

Teig stopped a moment on the threshold until the tramp of her feet had died away; then he made a hollow of his two hands and called across the road:

"Hey, there, Barney, will ye come over for a sup?"

9. The Holy Lake

A TALE LONG REMEMBERED IN THE DOLOMITES

Sing, Brother

What Eve is this?
Come ye, proclaim
A blessed day, a hallowed reign.
Sing, brother, through Jerusalem,
The Christ is born in Bethlehem!

What Star is this
With pure, white beam?
It shines upon a manger mean.
Sing, brother, through Jerusalem,
The Christ is born in Bethlehem!

What City this?
'Tis Judah's own,
A fitting birthplace and a throne.
Sing, brother, through Jerusalem,
The Christ is born in Bethlehem!

What Mother this?
A Virgin-maid,
Alone she bears Him, unafraid.
Sing, brother, through Jerusalem,
The Christ is born in Bethlehem!

Who is this Christ?
A Saviour born,
He beareth peace to the battle-torn.
Sing, brother, through Jerusalem,
The Christ is born in Bethlehem!

9. The Holy Lake

IT lies high up in the Dolomites in a straight line between Innsbruck and Verona. The water is clear, it carries on its cold blue surface the impression of crystal glass, an impression that if you should look through it you could see something. And you would, if the day were clear and still. If you should stand on one of those high places surmounting the lake, you would see, far down, a drowned village lying peacefully there in what was once a green valley.

Long ago there were silver mines about the village. Those who came to work them grew rich. It was fabulous how rich they grew. They put up houses far finer than any other village could boast of. They built a large church—far too large to hold the number of people in the village, with far too towering a steeple to keep guardianship over the shrunken souls that dwelt beneath it. For the people of the village lived by the vast tons of silver they mined; they lived for the silver. They threw away everything made of the baser metals and replaced these with silver. They ate from silver dishes; they drank from silver mugs; they burned their candles in silver sticks; they wore silver buttons and silver buckles. Their salutations were no longer: "Good-day," or "God keep you," but "God give you more silver." It was only in this greeting that God got into their lives at all.

And yet it seemed as if God must have heard their daily greeting, and was pleased by it. For no sooner did one vein of silver in a mine run out than a new vein was discovered. There seemed no end to the wealth of the mountains. And at night, of a full, high moon, the villagers would point to one of the many waterfalls that came cascading down the sides of the mountains, fed abundantly by the melting glaciers and snows, and say: "See—even our brooks run silver." And this seemed true.

They became proud and scornful, the people of the village, proud and scornful of the people of other villages, of all their neighbours in the Dolomites. It was as if the world around them had no importance; as if nothing were good enough or fine enough that they had not bought with their silver or had not made out of it.

Now pride and scorn are poor bedfellows. They will turn a good man into an empty-headed fool. If there is no longer need of earning daily bread, no longer need of counting the busy hours of the day that life might be wise and diligent, then the empty-headed fool becomes a man both vicious and greedy—a baser metal himself, and good for little but scrapping.

They became great eaters in the village, eaters of fine foods brought over the mountain on donkey-back and in lumbering carts. They became great drinkers. Not content with the wine from neighbouring vineyards, they must have casks of the best brought from wherever the world made it. So they ate much and drank much and were exceedingly merry, or thought they were. Every day became a holiday and a feast day; and when a real holiday came they had to whip it up into a time of wild orgy that they might put upon it the extra importance it should have. Saints' days, holy days, lost all meaning for them beyond the table, the wine cask, the gaming and the dancing. Although they paid a priest well to keep the Sabbath for them, they kept little of it for themselves.

Many years went by. Sons born to drinking fathers became good drinkers in their turn; daughters born to vain, light-minded mothers became flirts and wantons. Generations can build a village or blight it. And this one, in its green valley, became blighted.

Now of all the seasons of the year which offered the greatest number of days for celebration and the most abundant excuse for wanton gaiety was the Christmas season. In the streets as well as the houses the people caroused. They brought their wine casks in sleighs into the market square; they poured red wine not only down their own throats but down the throats of their servants, their horses, and even their game cockerels. The air was filled with raucous laughter, vulgar joking, ribald singing. Night became day and day night; and so the Eve of Christmas drew in.

Standing above the village, looking down on it, had you been there and so minded, you would have seen a picture that could well have been painted upon a card. Just such a village with the church spire and cross above it; snow binding hill and meadow together, making heavy the spruce and fir. And finally, as night fell, the snow coming down in large and lazy flakes, like powdered mica that you sprinkle on the card to make it seem truly Christmas. Everything looked soft and glinting, and showing through it were the copper lights of candles at the windows. If I had sent the card to you, you would have said: "What a lovely card! What a joyous and peaceful Christmas village." That is what you would have said.

At nightfall, with the snow, there came a young boy from the south. Rough clothes he wore, poorly clad, without cap, without stout mountain boots. His lips were blue with cold, his fingers pinched, his jacket tight about him. His eyes, blue as strawflowers, looked hollowed and hungry from under his heavy thatch of corn-coloured hair. He came laggardly down the last of the trails and reaching the village street he began at the farthest end to knock at every door.

Knock-knock-knock!

"What do you want?"

"Something to stay my hunger, a place to warm my heart."

"We are feasting tonight. We have no room for a stranger."

"I have come far. My home lies beyond the mountain, over the sea."

"Then go back to it!"

Knock-knock-knock!

"What do you want?"

"Something to stay my hunger, a place to warm my heart."

"We are feasting tonight. We have no room for a stranger."

"I have come far. My home lies beyond the mountains, over the sea."

"Then go back to it."

Knock-knock-knock!

Down the long length of the street on one side, back the long length on the other, the knocking went on. Some did not open the door at all. Some opened but to slam it again when the visitor was seen to be poor and a stranger.

Knock-knock-knock! It sounded louder as the night grew darker. It sounded above the shouting, the laughter, the singing. It came at last to fill the valley, echoing now from this side, now from that. It filled the very dome of Heaven, until it might have been a knocking at Heaven's door.

As the eve waxed into night, as the night waxed towards the coming Christmas Day, the swelling sound of the knocking was borne in upon the men and women, even upon the children tossing restlessly in their cots. They cried out in their sleep in a kind of fear, so that the peasant maids who tended them had to hush and bid them sleep again, promising again and again that nothing was amiss.

"What is it that we hear?" they asked.

"It is someone knocking at a door."

"Why isn't he let in? Why isn't he let in?"

"That is not our business. Go to sleep."

Their elders grew restless, likewise. A cup, filled anew with red wine, would be half lifted to the lips, then stayed while the drinker would listen for the knocking, which seemed no longer to come upon a door but rather upon his heart. Knock-knock-knock! Lovers held back the very words of love upon their lips to listen, then shuddering turned to their love-making again with faint hearts. Those who danced, those who threw dice, those who went back to the platters and goblets, paused oftener and oftener, until their half-befuddled minds could no longer keep off the sound that waxed and waned along the street, waxed and waned and waxed again.

"Curse you—throw the dice! Stop listening to that infernal knocking."

"The wine's grown sour; bring fresh."

"The lights are dim; fetch more candles."

"Your love sounds hollow."

"Your words have grown cold."

"The music's out of tune."

"This is no pavan—why do your feet stumble?"

"Send someone abroad to stop that cursed knocking."

Servants were dispatched at last. They bore heavy cudgels to enforce their command that the boy must stop his knocking and leave the village. But although they searched the street, looked well into each shadowed doorway and by-street, they found the village deserted save for one of their own people, going his drunken way. They returned to their masters and reported. Spirits rose. "He's gone, good riddance!" they shouted.

"Fill up the goblets!"

"I'll lay you thirty pieces of silver on the next throw of the dice."

But the boy—where was he? Finding every door in the village shut to him, he climbed to the nearest peasant hut and knocked there. An old grandmother came to the door, rubbing her hands. She saw the lonely child, the poor covering to his body, the hunger in his eyes, and the deep-rooted weariness in the droop of his young body.

"Poor lad, poor lad, come in." She drew him to the fire, pulling out a stool, pushing him down, that he might be closer to the warmth. "Hast eaten?" And not waiting for an answer she went for a bowl, to fill it with the hot broth that stood on the hearth. She cut the thick bread for him, and brought some goat's cheese. "It is thine, poor fare as it is. Nay, speak not until thou art fed."

She sat and watched him eat, clucking over every mouthful as one clucks to a young bird that eats out of one's hand. She twice filled the bowl with broth. And then, seeing the raggedness of his garments, she took off the jacket and with thread and needle and woollen patches she mended it, talking the while.

"Thou art alone. Hast thou come far? Hast thou no parents?"

"I have thee, Grandmother," said the boy.

"Surely, and I have thee. That is good. To be alone, to have one's kin gone, is a lonesome thing on Christmas Eve."

"Thou rememberest then what night it is?"

"Surely. It is a poor keeping we make of it in these parts. Soon will come the Midnight Mass, and I shall go. But it will be the same as other years—a sodden drunken crowd that falls asleep at their worship, that does not even know when the name of the blessed Christ and His Mother Mary are spoken. They cannot even cross themselves, they are so far gone with wine."

"I know," said the boy, "I know."

"Let us go to the church together. There will then be two worshippers who can pray with loving hearts."

"We stay here, Grandmother. We do not go."

The old woman looked at him, wondering. The light of the fire played about his golden hair, giving it a strange and spreading light. There was no more hunger in his eyes; but looking deep within them she saw austerity. They were no longer the eyes of the youth but the everlasting eyes of Eternal Judgment.

"Who art thou, lad?" asked the old woman.

"One thou hast known well; one thou hast known always, Grandmother."

And at that moment the bells from below rang out their summons to the Christmas Mass. "I have never missed going," sighed the old woman. "The bells on this Eve have made the pleasantest sound for me of all the year. They bring back to me the children, Gordo and Vinella, and the grandchildren, Maria, Lazar, and Rosa." She went to her window and looked down upon the church.

The boy stood beside her. "Come away from the window, Grandmother. If thou wilt come I give thee my promise thou shalt hear the bells ringing at Christmas Eve so long as thou livest and after. Come away. For what thou shalt presently see below is a sight too sad for thine eyes."

Already the bells had brought people tumbling out of their doors, tumbling and staggering, shouting and making all manner of loud, raucous sounds. "They should come quietly and reverently," mumbled the old woman.

"They will be quiet soon enough—let them shout now."

The old woman turned, her eyes grown suddenly wide with fear. "Who art thou?" she asked again. "Why will the wicked ones soon be quiet? What is to happen this night?"

"Be not afraid, Grandmother. There is a saying known to thee, no doubt: 'Yea, the light of the wicked shall be put out, and the spark of his fire shall not shine.' Come away!"

He drew her tenderly to the hearth, put fresh faggots on the fire, sat her in her chair, took the stool and sat at her feet, laid her hands peacefully upon her lap, crossing them with his own. And then he talked to her of his own mother, of their simple life at home, of his brothers and one sister. She saw, in what he told, her own life taking form as it had been, and felt again how good it had been, these things of living, of homely service, of preparing food, of hushing children, of making garments, of keeping a house tidy and pleasant. And while he talked, bringing the years home to her, she nodded and at last slept.

The sun was over all when she awoke Christmas Morning. She looked to find the boy but he had gone. Yet wood stood heaped plentifully upon the hearth, and food stood in abundance upon the shelves. The rose-bush at her window, which had borne only green leaves since summer, was now in full bloom.

"He is gone and I did not learn his name," she mumbled to herself regretfully, going to the window to wonder and feel and smell the beauty of the roses. Their fragrance almost overpowered her, dizzily she looked up and out. Snow bound together the mountains and the meadows, but below—below where, since she was born, the village had stood, there was no village. A lake covered the valley, filled it with crystal blue water, already turning to brittle ice.

"Yea, the light of the wicked shall be put out, and the spark of his fire shall not shine." She repeated the words slowly, as if saying them after him who had first spoken them. She passed her hands across her eyes, she spoke in awe: "I did not need to ask his name," she said.

And so the lake stands, the Holy Lake, it is called. In summer many come to see the village lying there under its clear waters. And on Christmas Eve those who pass, even far away, can still hear the ringing of the church bells, ringing the summons to the Christmas Midnight Mass. As the promise was made, so has the promise been kept.

10. The Crib of Bo'Bossu

FROM BRITTANY

Our Lady's Lullaby

[Old French]

This Holy Eve,
Let all receive
Thee in their hearts, I pray.
Oh, Little One,
The star hath shone.
Lullay—la—la—lullay!

Let here abide
This Christmastide
All peace, all joy, I pray.
Shepherd and king
Come worshipping.
Lullay—la—la—lullay!

Oh, dost Thou see
The Wise Men three
Lay down their gifts this day?
Sleep, Son of mine,
The World is Thine.
Lullay—la—la—lullay!

10. The Crib of Bo'Bossu

LISTEN, *mes enfants*, this is a tale for Noel—a tale from that part of France called Brittany, known among all people as the Country of Pardons. That is a good name; that tells you something already about the Breton folk, and I could tell you more. Do you know that all summer, along the sand dunes, the Korrigans dance in the moonlight? They are Celtic princesses who have lost their souls because they were born and died before the good tidings of the birth of Our Lord had been brought to them. Brittany is Celtic and the people are of deep faith, of light heart, of gay spirits. They are good workers. They mind their own business, and they expect you to mind yours.

On the Côtes-du-Nord there is the very ancient walled city of Saint-Malo. The Romans walled it, but they did not name it. It was named long afterwards for that good saint who was so gentle, so good, so mindful of lowly creatures, that one day when working in the field he put off his cloak, for the sun's heat was strong, and laid it on the brush. And when at eventide he went to cover himself again he found a wren had built her nest in the fold of the cloak, and rather than destroy the nest and the tiny bird's faith he left the coat to lie until the eggs were laid, the fledglings hatched and raised, while he went cold. That is something good to remember.

The city of Saint-Malo has a cathedral built of grey stone, as rugged, as massive, as eternal to stand as the Côtes-du-Nord itself. And there is something I must tell you of the city and the cathedral. The Breton navigator Jacques Cartier was born here. And in the cathedral, before the choir, he knelt for his last benediction before he sailed for the New World. A tablet tells one, so it must be true.

The Malouins are mostly sailors and fishermen and builders of boats. They are good men and unafraid on land or sea. For long now it has been the custom for them to keep the Eve of Noel with a celebration in the cathedral, before beginning the Christ Mass. This celebration is made that all should remember throughout the coming year the birth of Our Lord, and the placing of Our Lady on the Throne of Heaven. It is not enough that they should be told it happened thus and so, but they must hear again the birth proclaimed and see with their own eyes the manger.

Long before midnight the people of Saint-Malo gather. They come from the quays, from the yards, from the shops and the homes; they come in quiet, for this is a holy night. Long ago they bore torches through the twisted, narrow streets, leaving them outside, to enter in darkness—the whole cathedral dark save for the red eye of the oil lamp burning before the altar. Voices were hushed. No sound save for the brushing of feet against the flagging, the rustle of garments, the long indrawing of the breath in great expectancy.

This is the order of the celebration, *mes enfants,* and it has been changed little in the last three hundred years. In the darkness and the silence, high aloft, a young boy dressed in white, for he is the Angel of Glad Tidings, takes his place. Then out rolls the organ, and with voice high-soaring the angel sings:

Annuncio vobis gaudum magnum
Quia natus est hodie,
Salvator mundi,
Alleluia!

As by some breath of magic a thousand candles burst into flame, and all the children of Saint-Malo, robed in white, join the choir, bursting into jubilant song:

Gloria in excelsis Deo
Et in terra pax
Hominibus bene voluntates.
Alleluia!

Then come the shepherds. The number of them has grown with the long years. Sometimes they bring sheep with them from their folds, and one can hear the soft tinkling of the bells as they move up the long nave. They approach the choir where stands the manger, veiled. They sing their songs of praise, of peace. All hold their breath, for now the veil is drawn, the manger is disclosed, and all may look upon Our Lady, kneeling by the crib wherein lies the Babe, Lord Jesus. So beautiful it is! The children sing:

Alleluia, alleluia!
Christus natus hodie!

The church bells over all the city ring out for midnight. So begins the Christ Mass.

Now in the city there lived a hunchback whom everyone called Bo'Bossu. He worked down by the quays, an apprentice to the boat-builder Penhoël. There were a dozen apprentices like Bo'Bossu, but none so clever with the hands, none so quick to lay a keel, to shape a hull, or to carve with perfection the head or figure that often finished the prow of a large vessel. To Bo'Bossu was given the most delicate of the work; and he was happiest when he held wood or tool in his hands, when he was giving shape to something, could see it turn from a rough-hewn block or beam of oak or fir into a boat or some part of it before his eyes. The "Old One," Penhoël, and the other apprentices treated him kindly. Boys like himself, the apprentices looked up to him as the better craftsman; they watched often to see how he did this or that. The boat-builder gave Bo'Bossu a straw pallet in the corner of the boat-shed to sleep on, and fed him from his own table.

Of a truth Bo'Bossu was happy always at work, but to go abroad, that was another matter. On the streets Bo'Bossu met with jeers too often; and too often other boys, who were straight and strong as boys should be, pelted him with stones or refuse, laughing to see him take to his warped legs. That was funny—to see Bo'Bossu run for cover. And many believed, because the Malouins carry strange notions in their heads, that God's curse rested on the hunchback, that this curse had taken the form of misshapen legs and a hump.

He was a quiet boy, slow to move save when he was harried. He carried abroad always a white, frightened face—a sorry-looking boy. And when folk took time to look at him, which was rare, they thought: there goes one God has smitten. Never enough *potage* to fill his stomach, never enough love to fill his heart. All this was quite true, save that God had nothing to do with it.

Now Bo'Bossu loved the cathedral. He loved the very

weight and roughness of its structure, for there was strength as well as beauty in all of it. He loved the quiet hours when few came to pray. Saint Malo was his friend; Our Lady was his mother; the Lord Jesus was his brother; and to these in turn he would bring his aching heart and pour it out in slow, laboured speech. For his tongue had none of the skill that lay in his hands.

Before Our Lady he would kneel most often; he would plead for a small sliver, a shaving of Her love, that She might spare him this who knew no kin. That was why he went to the cathedral and bore the agony of his travels there and back, the fear of the stoning, the chasing, the abuse. Truly, to pray, to unburden the heart was worth this burden.

He did not know his own age, did Bo'Bossu. But he knew this much: he was no longer a child and not yet had he become a man. It was a gusty night of spring, he was kneeling after evensong in the cathedral before Our Lady, when the great, the magnificent idea came to him. On the Eve of Noel, now some four months past, he had been very near to the manger when the veil had been drawn, and he had seen for the first time how cheap, how crude was the fashioning of the manger in which the Babe, Lord Jesus, lay. Truly a poor affair to cradle the King of Kings. Had no one thought to make a better one? That was strange, for everything else about the celebration was rich and beautiful. So many candles, such stiff brocade and fine lace as Our Lady wore, and the priests put on their finest copes and stoles, beaded with seed-pearls and sewn with gold. And yet the Babe lay in a poor and roughly made crib.

That was the magnificent idea—that he should spend every precious moment of his spare time and make a fine one for the Blessed Babe. He would carve it, polish it, put all his skill into making it supremely fine. It would be a work of love for all the cathedral, a work to touch the heart.

He began to gather bits of wood left from the boats, good for nothing but to light the fires. He hid these under his straw pallet. When there were enough, he drew roughly with charcoal on the shed wall his design for the crib. It should be like a little boat, but with two prows, each with an angel as figure-head. It should have a wreath of ilex leaves about the gunwale, intertwined with the blossoms of the field lily. With the crib conceived, there remained only to win time for the work. He worked far into the long evenings; he worked at full of moon; he rose an hour before time for morning coffee. His own working hours for the Old One were long enough to tire; but this was work for love and he rested at it.

In the beginning there was no thought to make a bargain with Our Lady. But winter was at hand, he had gone again to pray at evensong and had been abused along the way worse than usual. The hurt in his heart was sharp as he knelt, and there rose to his lips his cry for help: "I am making a crib for Thy Son. It is for the coming Noel. It is beautiful. He will lie with comfort in it and be rocked, even as the great sea rocks the men of Saint-Malo. If Thou art pleased with it, I pray—oh, I pray—Thee to make me straight as other boys. But then—but then—I would lose my fear of the street. I could come with safety here—to Thee."

After that, until the very Eve of Noel, he never knelt before Our Lady that he did not think Her eyes were upon his hump, as if She noticed it now and felt for him a great compassion. Even in the dim light of the candles burning before Her, Bo'Bossu was certain that he saw compassion growing in Her eyes.

As Noel approached, as the crib neared its completion, he forgot hunger, he felt nothing of the cold, though his smock was thin and his breeches worn. A fever burned within him which kept him warm and satisfied. He sang at his work, as he swung the axe, as he smoothed with the spoke-shave, as he shaped and turned and ran in the copper bolts which held the planking. He had a pleasant voice and the other apprentices kept him singing. "Give us another *cantique* for Noel, Bo'Bossu," they would cry. He knew them all, that Bo'Bossu. He made of the long hours of the day a scrap of time that was soon gone. One song he always sang besides the carols and that was the song to the Earth which every Breton boy knows:

When Goodman Winter comes again—
    Sing to the Earth;
He covers up his blessed grain—
    Sing to the Earth.

Sleep quietly, Jean-the-wheat,
Till Spring and Winter meet;
Sing to the gentle Earth,
Mother of Bread, Mother of Birth.

A week—that was all there was left—seven days before the Eve of Noel. And there came a man from Dinan with an order for a new vessel for the fishing fleet. It must be ready for launching by early spring when the fleet set off for the Grand Banks, for Le Gran and Le Petit Manan.

That meant work not to be put off. The order came to begin the laying of the keel that day, and until the vessel was finished there must be no let nor hindrance to swift and skilful building.

Behind the straw pallet the crib lay hidden and almost finished; but the angel at one prow was not yet carved, and all had still to have much rubbing. So driven were the apprentices, so tired was Bo'Bossu at the end of the day that he threw himself down on his straw without eating. And so was it the next night and the next. An apprehension mounted in him with the fourth and the fifth day gone. Would he be too spent to finish the crib? He had made a promise to Our Lady. Would he break it? The singing was gone from his lips, and the others no longer urged him to sing. Time had become something terrible; there were a hundred hours to the day instead of the actual twelve they worked.

The dreams of the hunchback became full of terror and despair. Should he break this promise to Our Lady it would be no small offence. Bo'Bossu would wake in the night, crying out his protestations: "I came with it, but the boys in the streets threw themselves against me and the crib was dashed to the cobbles and lies there, broken," or: "The Old One has driven us every little moment and it is dark before I can work on the crib; and I have no candle to work by, no money to buy one." He had not even time to go to the cathedral to pray for time, a candle, some help, that the crib might be ready for the Eve.

On the Eve of Noel, according to the custom of all Malouins, Penhoël, the builder of boats, stopped work early. The apprentices went to their homes to dress themselves fittingly, and to smell the good smells of cooking for the feast that would follow the Mass. The building yard was deserted save for Bo'Bossu, who latched the door of the shed, took the crib from the hiding-place, and carried it to the west window where daylight would be entering the longest. But so little light: the sky was overcast and it looked as if the snow would be driving in from the sea by nightfall.

With frenzied fingers the hunchback started his carving. He had made the angel at the finished prow with a small open O of a mouth, that it might seem as if it were singing "Alleluia." The fire, that heated the shed none too well in winter, was out. Bo'Bossu could see his breath rise upwards in wreaths of cold mist. His hands were lumps of frozen flesh. It was as if he had never held a tool, never carved skilfully and well.

The day, having made up its mind to depart, went quickly.

Between watching it and dropping the tools, stopping to blow on his fingers, straightening a little the cramps in his back and legs, the first thing Bo'Bossu knew was that he could see to work no longer. With deep weariness, with despair, he put down his tool and leaned his poor twisted body on the bench. "I can do no more, Holy Mother, I can do no more!" He made of it a kind of chant, saying it over and over, making of it an outlet for his suffering.

And so it came about that he did not hear the latch of the shed lift, the sound of light, sandalled feet walking; nor anything at all, until a hand touched his shoulder and a voice said: "Give me the chisel. Thou hast worked long. Sleep, I will do it for thee."

The hunchback turned at the speaking. Beside him stood a boy his own age, his own height, had he been straight. He was clothed in a tunic that came almost to his ankles, so that Bo'Bossu thought him at first a novice. But the tunic was blue as the boy's eyes, which were blue as myrtle. A metal belt of strange workmanship held it about the waist. The boy's hair was yellow as a candle-flame; and to Bo'Bossu it seemed to cast light—like a candle. At least the shed seemed not as dark as it had been.

Long they looked at each other, the boy who was whole and the boy who was not. "Canst thou carve?" asked Bo'-Bossu. "Canst thou see to work?"

"Surely. There will be light enough to finish. Thou art very weary, sleep."

Amazed that he should trust another with this important

and holy thing, the hunchback went stupidly to his pallet, threw himself down, and was at once asleep.

The bells, ringing for the celebration, were what wakened him. He rose drugged with sleep, only to start in a kind of panic to his feet. "It is too late," he cried, and stumbled over to the bench. There he stood in wonder, for without wick or candle there was a wide circle of light about the strange boy, and in that light his hands were giving a last polish to the finished crib. Like rich satin it shone. For a long moment Bo'Bossu could not speak. Greater than the wonder of the light was the marvel of the workmanship. Although the crib was of his planning and his execution it was as if the holy hands of the Creator had touched it, making it perfect. "Who art thou?" asked Bo'Bossu.

The boy put down his cloth. "An apprentice, even as thyself. I work for my father."

The hunchback gave his twisted shoulders a shrug of hopelessness. "It is too late," he said again. "They will already have laid the Holy Babe in His crib. It is not for me to go behind the veil."

"It is not too late," said the boy. "Come, we will go together."

Together they bore the crib that was shaped like a small boat, with two prows and an angel at each prow, that had a garland of ilex leaves with lilies all around the gunwale, that was so heavy when Bo'Bossu bore it alone he could hardly lift it, but which was now no more than a feather's weight carried by the two.

They entered through the door of the priests and found their way through the darkness to where the manger was waiting. They put down the crib, and the boy nodded at Bo'Bossu and said: "Lift the Little One into thy crib and I will take away the other."

Clumsily the hunchback knelt. Humbly he reached for the little figure of the Blessed Babe and lifted it, smoothing out the long blue swaddling robe, straightening the tiny golden halo about its head. He had put the straw into the boat-crib, and carefully, on this, he laid the Babe.

Then it was that the greatest of all wonders of that holy Eve came to pass for Bo'Bossu. For as he placed the Lord Jesus in the crib the Babe opened His eyes. He smiled. It was a smile Bo'Bossu knew. The Babe's eyes were blue as myrtle. His hair was as yellow as a candle's flame. "Thou art the boy, and yet not grown as he. The boy is truly Thee, and yet not small as Thou art." The hunchback spoke the words in awe, with little understanding. He raised his eyes and saw that Our Lady was smiling even as the Babe. Not the figure of Our Lady, you understand, but, yes, Her own living self, come down to earth for that one holy Eve of Noel; come down to bless Bo'Bossu the hunchback.

From far aloft came the voice of the boy who was the angel:

Annuncio vobis gaudum magnum
Quia natus est hodie,
Salvator mundi,
Alleluia!

He was singing to the very dome of the cathedral—to the very dome of Heaven. Beyond the veil a thousand candles burst into flame and children's voices took up the "Gloria." The veil was drawn. The people of Saint-Malo held their silence for fear of breathing. For there beside the manger knelt Bo'Bossu—and yet not Bo'Bossu. They saw the new crib, a miracle of wonder, wherein lay the Babe so like a living babe that that, likewise, was a miracle.

From that night the hunchback walked the streets of Saint-Malo straight and strong like all Breton boys. The Malouins gave him a new name—the name of Jean, after that favourite disciple of the Lord Jesus. Throughout the singing of the Christ Mass for many years they pointed to the crib that was a small boat, with two prows and an angel at each one. They told the story of Bo'Bossu to their children and their children's children.

11. The Three Kings Ride

A TALE OF MANY CENTURIES

An Old Latin Carol to the Kings

Sing of desert and forest and far distant places;
Sing of all nations and sing of all races;
Sing of that Light which now shines on all faces;
Cum Virgine Maria.

Sing of the Ear of the World—what it heareth;
Sing of the Heart of the World—what it feareth;
Sing of the Soul of the World—what it beareth;
Cum Virgine Maria.

Sing, Eastern Monarchs, ye Chaldeans three;
Sing of thy gifts which ye bear in plentee;
Sing, while ye worship on thy bended knee;
Cum Virgine Maria.

Sing of this Maid who hath born the Messiah;
Sing of the purity, faith, and the fire
Which burns in Her heart for the Son and the Sire;
Haec Virgine Maria.

11. The Three Kings Ride

THE Roman, Aelius Antoninus, had been a soldier, boy and man, all his life. He had known nothing else but fighting. He had served under Hadrian while he was praetor, and later when he was Emperor. At the end of his service he had been promoted to senior centurion and had been sent at last to that legionaries' camp city of Italica in Spain which was founded by the first Scipio Africanus. Here he lived comfortably. The baths were the best, the fighting in the arena as good as a Roman could ask. The fiercest beasts were brought from Africa, the Libyan desert, the highlands of Asia; they gave the gladiators good combat.

But as he grew old Antoninus grew tired and slightly bored with comfortable living. Life had been good, campaigning. What had he not seen? What had he not done? Whom had he not fought? He had led his cohorts well under Hadrian, and it had been a lusty, stormy, outstriding life, knowing something of defeat but more of victory. The gods had been good to him, and he had not done ill by them. But time came when he grew restless watching one more lion fighting his last fight. He found himself spending more and more time in the baths, yawning away good hours of a still good life.

Restlessness drove him to the road. He travelled up and down the ancient river Baetis, that he might see all of the Roman province. He found children along the way; and as there were few in Italica, as he had had none of his own, they interested him, especially the lads. He spent much time at Hispalis, which is now the city of Seville, loitering in the public square, watching the boys playing with their small javelins, throwing their discuses. He picked out a certain one named Flavius, a boy of ten; and him he bound in a growing friendship because of the tales he had to tell, the wonder and variety of them. He told of the Britons on their island across from Gaul. He told of the far Rhine, of the Parthians, of what he had seen in Asia Minor, of Antioch and Athens, Thebes and the Nile. And he told of that far-away city of Jerusalem and the strange tribes of the Jews, whom the Romans had conquered.

It happened on a day in early April that Antoninus brought the lad Flavius to Italica to see the yearly festival for the Great Mother of the Gods. In the arena were to be games and chariot races, and slaves throughout the empire were coming to wrestle.

"Who is this Great Mother?" asked the lad. "I do not rightly know her."

"In truth she is not a Roman goddess—not as we claim Ceres and Juno. But we, the army, worship her with great honour. The Sibylline Books have prophesied of her. Like Mithra, we have found it well not to slight her. She is over the winds, the sea, the earth, and all creation. She gave us victory over the Mauretanians without a doubt."

"I will take Mars and Vulcan," said the lad contentedly. "What can they not do? And for a goddess—give me Minerva, O Antoninus."

"It is well to pray and make sacrifices to all. We slaughtered a six-year-old bull to the Great Mother this day at dawn. The smoke of it filled the heavens, the blood propitiated the ground well. We should have a fine harvest."

"There are too many gods," said the lad wearily. "I cannot remember them all, and who has the olive branch and who the pine, and what they best like for sacrifice. It would be better if they all went but Father Jupiter, and he alone took care of us."

"Mind thy tongue, boy. Even now the gods may be listening!"

The chariot races had begun. They watched the winner

crowned, and Flavius, still confused over the Great Mother, plied his questions further: "Is she mother over Jupiter?"

"I have told you, she is mother over all the gods. The only one. . . ." A look of perplexity passed over the big soldier's face, then a smile broke the grim line of his mouth. "I have told thee of Jerusalem and the Jews. I was with the Emperor there when he ordered the city rebuilt and saw many shows in the arena. It is not as it is here—the fights. There the gladiators combat prisoners; and the lions, the leopards, and the tigers fight with a strange people called Christians."

"I have never heard of them," said Flavius.

" 'Tis as well." The centurion shrugged his shoulders as if to dismiss all thought save that which bore upon the festival. A great procession was forming in the arena. The music of flute, tympan, and cymbal, lute and tambourine sounded. Those who marched were garlanded, and there were many dancers. And then a dark blot of dun colour in the midst of the saffrons, blues, crimsons, and greens of the tunics caught the eye of the Roman centurion, and he laid a compelling hand on the lad beside him. "Look. There are Christians. Those towards the end of the procession, chained together. They have brought them here from Rome, no doubt, to force them to do honour to the Great Mother. A good joke." And Antoninus threw back his head and bellowed laughter.

But the lad understood nothing of this joke. "Tell me, O Antoninus, why is it so funny?"

"Because the Christians have a great mother of their own.

I heard of her in Jerusalem. It will go against the spleen of those four to worship another."

The dancing had begun. Swaying, singing, shouting, playing, the procession advanced until the chained men had come directly below the centurion and the lad. "There is nothing fierce in them," Flavius said as if disappointed. "Is it such as these who fight the lions?"

Again Antoninus bellowed. "They fight not. It is against their belief. They stand like stuffed sacks and let the beasts slaughter them."

Without knowing it the lad sighed. "At that rate, there will soon be no more of them."

The big soldier patted him approvingly: "Thou hast some of thy Minerva's wisdom. They cannot last out the empire."

"And this mother that they worship—what is her emblem? What sacrifices to her do they make? Where have they set up her altar?"

The centurion's laughter was running low; he mixed it with his words: "Sacrifices! Altar! Rome would tear it down had it found one. They worship in secret. It is strange that any worship could have come out of such a simple, everyday affair. She was the mother of a man born in Judea, a Jew. They crucified him—the Roman governor ordered it because the Jews, his own people, demanded it. It happened little more than a hundred years ago. I talked with a Roman legionary whose grandsire had seen the crucifixion. The man had set himself above the priests as a kind of prince and saviour of the world; mayhap he called himself the son of a god, I forget. So when he was crucified all looked for some great heavenly omen or deed to be enacted, for Jehovah, the god of the Jews, to come down and take this one, his son, from the cross."

"Did nothing happen?"

"Nothing. They buried him. His mother wept. A few of his followers took his body to a tomb. That was all."

"What was her name?"

"I have forgotten, if I ever knew." He pulled at the lad's sleeve. "Look—look at the Christians now. They will whip them till they kneel in worship before the Great Mother. I doubt not they will whip them till they die." And Aelius Antoninus, the senior centurion, threw back his great head, pounded his chest with delight, and bellowed his laughter again so that all heard. It rang across the arena and one of the chained and flogged men in dun-coloured robes turned his eyes towards him, raised one shackled hand, and pointing lean fingers upwards he made the sign of a cross. A cross in the air between himself, the laughter, and the man who had made it.

The lad watching shivered. "I feel cold," he said. "The air is sharp for April."

A great harvest was reaped in Baetica that fall. All remembered how tremendous was the festival celebrated for the Great Mother of all the gods and doubted not that having Christian blood to mix with bull's blood had propitiated well the goddess.

The Three Kings Ride

Winter came cold for the south of Spain. December was far gone and the time approached for the ending of the Saturnalia, the last day of the revels. The Roman centurion departed early from the camp for Hispalis. He rode along the river-front, with night coming on. There was a young crescent moon in the sky and all was clear and fair. The spirits of Aelius Antoninus rose. By years he might be a man growing old, but in feeling he was still young, strong, full of the good lusty appetite for life and all it held. He was thinking that he might live to see the rounding of the century. That would be something.

The padding of soft feet behind him roused him from his reverie. He drew up to see who these were, overtaking him. His horse under him began to shake like aspen, and for one who had been a Roman legionary he felt a strange cold gripping about the heart. For coming towards him on three gigantic camels were men the like of which he had never seen in all his marching with the Roman army of conquest.

The pale thin curve of the moon's light picked out every detail of their splendour. Their robes were richer than any emperor's. Jewels of great brilliance caught them together at throat and belt. Each rider wore a crown—the magnificence of these crowns surpassed anything Antoninus had seen in Egypt, in Persia, in Greece, in the far reaches of the Euphrates.

The camels were caparisoned with rich cloths and harness. As they drew abreast, the Roman could see that each King—or so he took them to be—carried in his hand a jewelled casket. Albeit a great man himself, and his horse a mount of no mean stature, he had to look well up to see their faces. One was dark, one black as a Nubian, one as fair as a Greek. "Who are ye? Whence come ye? Whither go ye?" the Roman asked with the voice of Roman authority.

"I am Melchior, a King from Nubia and Arabia, wherein lies gold. Behold I bring it as my gift." He held up the jewelled casket.

"I am Balthasar, a King from Tarsis and the Isle of Egriswilla, wherein grows myrrh."

"I am Gaspar, a King from India and Saba, land of spices. I bring frankincense. Together we ride to Bethlehem in Judea."

"On camels!" Antoninus let out prodigious laughter. "Ye will be in your graves before ye reach there." And then his mouth snapped together, making a grim line. The words he next spoke were those of a Roman soldier. "Come ye to make trouble? Know this: the Roman empire allows no interference. Our power is supreme. What business takes ye into Judea?"

Antoninus's quick eyes caught the look that passed from King to King, a secret look. It angered him. "Speak up, ye Kings from the East. What business takes ye to Judea?"

"To bear gifts. Look—I bring gold."

"And I, frankincense."

"And I, myrrh, to the King of Kings."

Again each King held up his jewelled casket.

A look of greater bewilderment covered the face of the

Roman. "What mean ye—the King of Kings? The birth of such a one was prophesied in Herod's time—to be born in Judea. But He was crucified a hundred years ago. The man is dead, forgotten."

Again the secret and wise look passed from King to King. Melchior spoke. "And what is a hundred years? God Himself hath said a thousand years shall be even as a day. We ride tonight to the manger where Jesus lies, even as we rode when He was born. We bear those gifts we first brought Him. So shall it always be. Until the world grows too old to bear men longer on its surface, we, Three Kings, ride to worship Him, our Lord Jesus."

Here was a joke the magnitude of which Antoninus had never in his entire life experienced before. Three Kings riding to worship a new-born baby who had grown to manhood, been crucified, died, and was buried over a hundred years ago. Three Kings still riding! Here was a joke to regale the camp with when he returned on the morrow. Suppressing his mirth the Roman said: "He has been a man dead these many years, and yet he becomes a babe that you may have him to worship. Your Christian god works miracles and this is one no doubt. Our Roman gods can do much—much—but once born and grown they do not become babies again. Venus does not go back to her sea-shell; Hercules does not go back to his cradle to strangle the serpent. Ha-ha-ha-ha, ho-ho-ho-ho!" His laughter shattered the air.

They let him have his fill of it; then Melchior spoke again: "That is thrice thou hast laughed, Aelius Antoninus the

Roman! The counting has been made against thee. Thou shalt live until thou hast expiated each laugh. Thou shalt live until thou too shalt kneel beside the Babe and worship Him."

The Kings rode on into the night. The Roman watched them go, sobered for the moment, then amazed. That last night of the Saturnalia had no flavour for him. The next day he told of his preposterous encounter to his familiars at the camp but the joke tasted foully to him, and the veterans insisted he had been deluded by too much strong wine.

Years passed. Aelius Antoninus began to mark their toll, which was as nothing for him. Others, those who had been retired at Italica with him and were of the same age, he watched grow feeble, and at last be carried to their graves. Yet time aged him not at all. He watched Flavius grow into manhood, reach prime, age, and be buried; yet his own body remained unstooped, his stride vigorous, his muscles sound. It was incredible. It was a curse! A kind of terror slowly filled him which lingered even in his sleep.

The soldiers in the camp had long since avoided him. The new governor coming from Rome, where Marcus Aurelius was now Emperor, had stricken his name from the records as one long since dead. Hearing this he left Italica and became a wanderer on the face of the earth. Every temple he passed —to whatever pagan god it had been erected—he stopped to make sacrifice and prayer. He sought out those cities which were besieged and joined the attacking army, thrusting himself into the front ranks, praying that some lance, some stone from a cross-bow might end his life. He visited those cities stricken with the plague. He helped to nurse the sick, to bury the dead; he drew in great draughts of the death-infested air, hoping one breath would bring him to his end. Yet all these things he survived.

A hundred years passed. Homesickness drove him back to Baetica, to the camp, to find the might of Rome weakening. He rode again upon the river road that last night of the Saturnalia. Would they come—would they ride, those Kings? Throughout the hundred years he still scoffed at all save pagan gods. Even with death withheld, he doubted that the Kings would come again.

But even as before he heard the padding of camels' feet behind him. He turned to meet again the splendour of the Kings, to see each carrying the golden casket in his hands, come as before. The Kings hailed him. "Peace be with thee, brother."

Anger mounted hot within him. He thrust his chin at them in fierce scorn: "And still ye ride?"

"As we shall always ride."

"And the babe is born again?"

"As He shall always be re-born this blessed season."

"A fig for your babes!" And the Roman laughed again long and hard, but with a hollowness that struck upon his heart. He watched them ride into the night and turned his horse back to the camp, but having no longer a place within he rode on northwards.

How can I tell you all that befell the Roman, Aelius Antoninus? He journeyed into Britain and watched the Druids worship their god, the sun. He found the gods of the Gauls much the same as his own. He took passage to Africa to see where old Carthage had been. The boat was shipwrecked and all lost save himself. He came back to Spain to find the Vandals ruling it; and met again the Three Kings and laughed and laughed so that the wind caught up his laughter and seemed to carry it throughout the world.

When next he came he found the Goths overrunning Spain. The Boldmen, they were called, mighty, barbaric, and conquering, good warriors but without the culture that Rome had brought. He became a ghost which went about visible to all, pointed out for the ancientness of his armour, and for the mystery which clung to him. Wherever he went his speech was forever betraying him. The Boldmen brought him into their halls, bade him to their feasting, made him welcome until unwittingly he spoke of Hadrian, of the campaign against the Britons; and then a silence fell and even Alaric the King was seen to draw away from him in a kind of fearful amazement.

Like the swinging of a great pendulum the centuries went on. He came again to Spain and found the Goths gone and the Arabs everywhere. They had set up a strong kingdom in the south, had made of the Roman city Hispalis a Moorish one. He learned of a new god, his name was Allah, and of his prophet Mohammed. When he met the Kings upon the road he threw these names at them. "By Jupiter, ride into their city—look at their mosques—hear them calling to their god from the high towers, and then tell me if you keep on to Judea?"

"We ride," said the Kings.

"So ye still worship that Jesus, even while a new King has come to claim the world. Fools—fools—fools!" And he shook his fists in a mighty anger at them.

Five centuries, six centuries, and still Aelius Antoninus grew not one year older. He saw the Jews come into trade and grow rich. He stopped a certain important one named Isadore in the street and asked: "Have you heard of one of your own people by the name of Jesus?"

"There are many called by that name."

"This one was born in Bethlehem, lived, and was crucified. Tell me is he a King?"

The Jew shook his head. "He claimed to be a King, even the Messiah, but he was false."

That year the Roman waited long upon the road for the Kings, to fling this thing a Jew himself had said concerning Jesus. But night after night passed. Instead of coming at the end of the old Saturnalia, it was twelve days afterwards before he heard the padding of the camels' feet on the road behind him, and in a surge of victorious scorn he blocked their way. "I salute you in the name of Jupiter, Hercules, Mars, Mithras, Allah—yea, even Jehovah, but never in the name of Jesus." He spat upon the ground. "Even his race denies him. Hear what the Jew Isadore saith!" And he told. "Now whither ride ye?"

"To Bethlehem, in Judea."

"But ye are late. Ye will get there only to find him crucified." And the Roman laughed.

"We will find him a babe of thirteen days. Already the church celebrates our day—the Day of the Three Kings—the day we reach Bethlehem. So it shall be upon that day we henceforth ride, not upon the eve of His birth." And they passed on into the night.

Seven centuries—he saw Charlemagne and the Franks marching against the Arabs. He saw the establishing of a Christian kingdom following a Mohammedan one. He watched churches being built upon the mosques, bell-towers above minarets, Mass said instead of the muezzin call to prayers, *prie-dieux* instead of prayer-rugs. And now, behold, the very images of Jesus filled the churches—Jesus and His Mother. Christians were on the streets, Christians on the seas, Christians marching, marching, marching, everywhere.

The name of Díaz of Bivar, the great Christian warrior, was heard on every lip; the name of the Blessed Santiago was whispered wherever a Christian army marched, and the battle cry "For God, Jesus, and Mary!" rang out through Spain. Ferdinand the Saint had come to rule. Nearly twelve hundred years had gone since that first night the Kings rode. Aelius Antoninus waited again upon the road. He now knew the name of this night on the Christian calendar—it was called the Eve of the Epiphany. So long had it been since he had heard the names of the ancient gods spoken that he could recall them only with great difficulty. No temple was left standing to them, all worship of them had crumbled. He had stood outside the doors of some of the churches and heard something of this new worship. Strange words took form—Love—Peace—Mercy—Life—Justice. He heard low mumblings of sacrifice, but could not understand the nature of it. No longer were creatures slaughtered on the altar, no bringing of young lambs or cocks. Now there was talk of giving away all one had to the poor, of forgiving an enemy, of laying down a life for a friend. Strange teachings!

But he would have more of it. This time he would question the Kings.

They came, and again there hung in the western sky a young crescent moon. He heard the padding of the camels. He drew to the side of the road, dismounting, to wait for the Kings to stop. But the Kings rôde on. "I salute ye!" he cried, running beside the camel of Melchior. "Stop! I command! I would have speech with ye!"

"We cannot stop. Tonight we make haste. Tonight we keep tryst with our Lord Jesus yonder."

But Antoninus caught at the bridle. "Wait, I must have speech with ye. Another hundred years and I shall be mad. Hark ye, I cannot live longer. Confusion has come upon me. My body is a curse; my heart has withered. I would lie down and sleep in eternal death."

"There is no eternal death."

"You mean there is Olympus for the brave?"

"We mean there is a heaven, call it what you will, for souls who find their salvation."

"But ye have cursed mine."

"Thou hast laughed the curse upon thyself. Thou must bear it till—" The words were lost to the Roman. His breath was coming in choking gasps. It seemed as if the camels were outstriding the air itself. But he would not let go of the bridle; he would not lose the Kings, not again. He would run beside them till he dropped, till death took him.

They came to the bridge spanning a great muddy river. And on the bridge were massed such a crowd as had never filled the square of the city for the feast of Saturn, or for the Great Mother, or for Father Jupiter himself. Rich and poor, noble and peasant. Torches flared to heaven. Musicians lined the way. Children cast flowers on the bridge—white jasmine, claveles, roses. And as the Kings came there arose such a shouting as shook the very stars and made them fall: "Melchior, Gaspar, Balthasar! The Kings ride!"

They rode to the church which had been an Arab mosque. As the great doors swung open, a hush so profound caught up the crowd and held it that one could hear a new-born babe sigh, that one could hear an angel bending low from Heaven's own gate to listen, that one could hear the curving of Mary's lips in a smile. So was it.

The Kings entered first; Aelius Antoninus the Roman strode hard upon their heels. They traversed a Christian nave between what had once been a line of Moorish arches supporting the roof. They came to the high altar, lighted by towering candles, and there was built the coarse, rude stall—the like of which might be found in any eastern stable. An ox stood there, a small grey donkey. A man leaned upon his staff, his heavy beard of black half covering his face. A woman in a robe of blue knelt beside the ox's manger, filled with hay. And there within lay the Babe, now thirteen days of age. All living—all everlasting!

The Kings knelt. The Roman knelt, unknowing what he did. He heard the Kings give salutation: "Peace be unto Thee, Blessed Mother of Jesus; and peace unto Thy Son."

He heard the low, sweet voice of this Great Mother: "Peace be unto ye, O Kings."

Then came the salutation to the Babe: "Peace be unto Thee, Emanuel, now and forever more. As Thou art now so Thou shalt always be—King of all Kings, Saviour of all Saviours—Prince of Peace!"

Drawing himself closer upon his knees, Aelius Antoninus the Roman found himself giving the salutation: "Peace be unto Thee, Jesus of Bethlehem. I salute Thee above Jupiter—above Mithras, above Allah, above all gods. May Thy reign be eternal and supreme."

And so did Aelius Antoninus find death at last. Yet abroad, on the face of many countries, in the memory of many people, he left a legend. The legend of a Roman centurion, ageless and a wanderer, seen in this country and in that, upon the mountain fastnesses, and upon the seas, marked throughout so many centuries that the counting has not been kept absolute. But of all places Spain knew him best. And so God rest his soul!

12. A Candle for Saint Bridget

A MODERN FOLKTALE

All Mothers Speak to Mary

Send forth the star;
And, Mary, take His hand—
He may not understand
How changed we are.
Light towering candles, rim
The earth with them;
Let angels sing "Amen"
To His birth-hymn.
Let Thy sweet laughter
When He was born
Fill this dark morn—
Sky-rafter to rafter.

Mary, thou canst see
Between the suns
The road that runs
From manger to Calvary.
Let Him not fear our dole
Of hate and gall;
He is too small
For agony of soul.
Make then His coming bright
On earth; let every door
Swing wide with peace; nor
Let one evil thing blot out the night.

12. A Candle for Saint Bridget

HERE is a personal Christmas story. Yet it is pure folktale. It pulses with the faith and the feeling of simple people; it has the background that is indigenous to all folk-telling. It begins many years ago in Ireland; and the words of old Michael Barron come back to me as I write: "Aye, it takes more than a handful of years for a good tale to ripen."

I went to Ireland to follow the trail of folk and fairy lore, to search out the best living storytellers from Malin Head to County Cork. That is how I came to find Michael Barron in his cabin on the moors in Donegal. The cabin was perched alone at the borderland where the moors stop and the jagged, sea-hewn cliffs of the Ulster coast begin. East, west, north, and south there wasn't another sign of life except the sea gulls and mews, circling and screaming the lee long day.

Michael was among the last of the seanachies; by far the oldest, I had been told, and the most knowledgeable. I found him on a day in midsummer, sitting outside the cabin sunning himself. He was pulling at an empty cuddy pipe for solace. He had not had tobacco to fill it since spring. He seemed centuries old—a human being over whom time had command no longer. His flesh had shrunken from his frame, and over it the skin was as brown and wrinkled as one of our butternuts. His eyes were of that pale opaque blue of extreme age; they held the childish look of perpetual inquiry. His lips were shirred around the stem of his pipe; from under his vagabond hat showed a thatch of colourless hair. I never saw Michael without his hat and his pipe, indoors or out.

His greeting was characteristic of those who still speak Gaelic: "God and Mary welcome ye. 'Tis a brave day." Then he took out his pipe, sucked at the air a moment, and asked: "Might ye be the Wee One?"

Having settled the fact of my identity he called in a high, quavering voice: "John—Delia—both of ye come out and bring the childher. Here's the Wee One, the Yankee lass we've been expecting the lee long time."

John and Delia came—his grandchildren; and the "childher" who flocked outside with them were Michael's great-grandchildren. It took no keen scrutiny to disclose the poverty that hung on them. A brood of half a dozen, aerach-shinned children, barely nourished; a sickly, stooping man with a cough, the beaten look in his eyes; a woman gaunt as poverty, flat-breasted, as bleached as the corn in November, wearing a rag of a dress and no shoes; and last of all Michael himself, an old man living beyond his time and usefulness, taking a share of the scant food that might have gone into the stomachs of the children. All these housed in a two-room cabin bare of everything but the bones of necessity. Such were Michael Barron and his kindred; yet I would travel the length and the breadth of Ireland today to find Michael Barron again.

The meal-chest was empty; the last pinch of tea had gone into the pot for breakfast, the last potatoes had been cooked that morning. This I learned afterwards. With that hospitality that acknowledges no defeat, Delia hung a fresh kettle over the hearth and set the pan warming against a baking of griddle bread. John and the oldest boy tramped to a cabin in the hollow a mile distant to ask the loan of tea and meal, and borrow a white egg from one of the hens, so that the stranger under their roof might not be sent away hungry.

That the lapse of time and the thin subterfuge might not be discovered, Michael Barron folded his hands with dignity and asked would I like to be hearing a tale, and would I like best to be hearing a *loidhe* about the Wandering of Oisin or a tale of the Blessed Saint Bridget?

I chose both. Whereupon, with a chuckle of delight, Michael whispered to Delia, who knelt at his side blowing the turf: "She has the right sense for listening to tales, and the heart, too. She might have Irish blood in her."

First he chanted the *loidhe* of Oisin. As I listened to those running minor cadences, rising, falling, in rhythmic perfection, I knew I was listening to a great traditional story-teller, one whose forebears had been bards at the court of the High King. His Gaelic was the purest I had ever heard, and afterwards Delia told me that a certain professor at Oxford had spent five successive summers there, brought a tent and camped out on the headlands above the sea, that he might be taught by the best Gaelic scholar in Ireland. "Aye, 'tis the truth," agreed Michael. "And what's more, Quiggan's grown to be a fair-to-middling scholar himself, the now."

We had the tale of Saint Bridget, then. The legend has been made immortal by Fiona Macleod in his stories of Iona. But I heard it first from Michael Barron that day. Before he had finished John had returned from his borrowings and Delia had the griddle bread mixed and baking. The brown, sweet smell of it filled the cabin as Michael's last words came like a lilting chorus: "So 'twas the Blessed Saint Bridget who came back to Iona, gone in her own thinking while a throstle sang; and yet in Time's reckoning it made a year and day. 'Twas herself told the Druids of that first Christmas and fetched the message of peace on earth. And she had the proof of what she was telling in the shawl she wore about her shoulders and in which she had cradled the wee Lord. For every thread in it was turned to gold, and the pattern of the weaving made the creatures in the byre at Bethlehem—ox and ass and lamb."

There was gooseberry jam to eat with the griddle bread, and tea long-steeped, black and bitter as sloe. The family made merry, as if the meal-chest were not empty and the food on the table borrowed. I had two half-crowns with me and slipped them into the fist of the "wee-est one" fast asleep in her cradle. On the way back I remember I made a special prayer to Saint Bridget that Delia would find the money before the baby woke and swallowed it. When I reached the little town at the hill's end I sent back the fillings for Michael's pipe by Mickey the postboy.

After that I came often to the cabin. Always Michael was ready with a new tale, or could be coaxed into telling again a favourite. Poverty no longer stalked the cabin; instead wonder came, and laughter, and we walked together the highway of good fellowship, whereon all walk who have known the sharing of good tales. Often at day's ending Michael would chuckle with delight and say: "Now ye have something to put in your head and fetch home with ye." And once he spoke plaintively: "If ye could write them down, the now, there'd be plenty of lads and lasses across the water thinking long for Ireland and the old tales. They'd be home-sick, just, to be hearing them."

Next to telling stories Michael Barron liked to be telling

about his grandchild Cassie, sister to Delia. She had gone to America, married a good man there, had two bonny children, and, like as not, would be bringing them back to Donegal a summer soon. Michael showed with pride Cassie's picture—a cheap, glazed photograph. But its lack of all art could not hide Cassie's Irish beauty, or the health and charm of the children. "Aye, they be's doing grand," was Michael Barron's comment.

I sailed late in October. The last person I went to see was Michael. He was watching for me from outside the cabin, even though the day was bitterly cold. Delia had wrapped him in an old quilt and a homespun shawl so that only his hat and pipe showed. I had not breasted the hill, however, before he saw me coming and was on his feet, waving me a welcome: "Sure, wasn't I telling Delia, just, ye'd be back for one more visit, to drink a last cup of tea and hear a last tale. Wasn't I telling Delia that!" He was like a child transported with delight, a child who can throw care and the morrow to the four winds and live in the contentment of today.

We gathered about the turf, our eyes red with the smoke from it, our hearts free as birds. Mickey the postboy dropped in bringing currants to bake in the griddle bread, and a pat of butter to spread thickly on it. We had not one story but many, and sat far into candle-time. And the last tale of all was the one about Saint Bridget. Delia sat with her foot on the cradle keeping the "wee-est one" hushed, while Michael took us over the hills again to Bethlehem. He brought us to the byre with its rude stalls; he showed us the crib with the hay filling it and the Babe asleep on it. He showed us Bridget gathering the Wee Lord to her breast, and he made us hear the first cradle-song crooned for Him. A few times, from far off, I have glimpsed Bethlehem; but never before nor since have I ever entered there.

Michael's last words still ring down the years: "Ye'll mind to find my Cassie—no matter whatever else ye fail to do. Tell her ye've seen Delia and the childher, and they be's doing grand. Tell her ye've seen her grandda, and he be's braver than anyone. Tell her that; and God and Mary go with ye."

When I sailed from Londonderry, Mickey the postboy sailed steerage. He was coming to America to find his fortune as many an Irish lad before him had done. I saw him on board several times, and just before landing I marked his eyes, already full of homesickness. He clung to me feverishly. "I might be coming soon to see ye. Maybe ye'd be a bit lonesome yourself for an Irish face."

I agreed that it was more than probable. But Mickey did not come. I made one attempt to find Cassie. At the address that Michael had given me the janitor told me she had moved away more than a year before. He referred me to possible neighbours who might know where she had gone, and to the corner grocer. After one or two more inquiries I gave up.

And this brings us to Christmas Eve of that year. I was very tired. The bed was strewn with packages, ribbon, seals, and there were half a dozen more packages to tie. Two gold pieces, one for our old Negro laundress, one for Ole Jensen, our janitor, lay on the corner of the bureau. I was wondering how to wrap them up when the telephone rang. The hallboy below reported a person to see me who would give no name but appeared "kinda hurried and nervous." A moment later Mickey the postboy stood on the threshold.

He was blue with cold; he twirled his cap uncomfortably. I asked him in but he shook his head. The gander had his tongue, as the Irish say. So I spoke: "Merry Christmas, Mickey. Like New York?"

He fumbled for his words: " 'Tisn't so good a Christmas —not for Michael Barron's Cassie. Ye mind Cassie?" His face was troubled; there was a gentle accusation in it, too, as if I should have found out Cassie for myself and not left it wholly to him.

"I looked for her." It was a lame excuse. "What is it, Mickey?"

"She be's in trouble, aye heavy trouble. Ye'll go with me to her the night." It was a command. I turned at the door to get my things when his voice halted me: "If ye've got some silver —a bit of money would come in mortal handy."

It was a bitter night. Mickey and I took the old elevated for the Battery. On the train he told me something of his search for Cassie. It had been fruitless until that day. He had gone into the Little Church of Saint Anthony early, to pray, and caught the half-glimpse of a face under a shawl that looked like Cassie. She had slipped out ahead of him but he followed, trailed her to a tenement, saw her go in. Then he waited, saw her come out again, hesitated this time, and lost her. He went back to the tenement and talked with her neighbour across the hall. Michael's own telling of what he heard was brief enough: "Her man's dead—dead a year. The long illness has eaten up their savings. She is after working now in a factory making skirts, paying the neighbour a shilling a day to look after the childher. But she can't earn enough to keep the wolf from the door. Back rent to pay and naught left for food or fixings. That's how it is. Fighting the wolf off and the wolf getting in at last."

We walked half a dozen blocks and turned into a smear of a street. The tenement sagged and smelled even in that clear, frosty air. A foul and dingy flare of gas lighted the hallways below. There were four flights to climb and Michael stumbled ahead, reached the top, and was knocking at a door before I had reached the end of the last flight.

The door opened. There stood Cassie in her black dress, a black shawl tight around her, her face gone white, a candle-end in her hand. I can still see the room behind her, ill lit as it was, and the red rings about her eyes from long crying. Mickey need not have told, nor the neighbour, of the sorrow and trouble that had come to Cassie; it was all written plainly in her face for the whole world to read. She looked out blankly into the dark hall at the two of us there. And then we saw her face lighten; there was a sharp expectancy in her voice: "Could it be someone from home—someone from the old country?" she asked.

She took a quick step, holding the candle closer to us. The

flame barely grazed Mickey's nose. She gave her breath a sudden intake, her words came in an awed whisper: "Holy God, if it isn't Wullie O'Neill's Mickey!" She leaned against the doorjamb to steady herself, while her voice took on strength: "Lar—lad—where did ye drop from this bitter night?"

Mickey pulled her into the room and I followed. His words ran together like huddling sheep. He explained himself; he explained me. He spoke messages from all in Donegal. And last of all he spoke of Michael Barron. "Your grandda's doing brave. She'll tell ye," and his thumb waggled at me. "She'll tell ye how the lee long summer she's been a-listening to Michael Barron's telling of tales, as brave a seanachie as ever he was. She'll tell ye that the tales are as thick on his tongue as ripe gooseberries on their bush." And he turned to me with impatience. "Aye, speak up—tell Cassie the words her heart's a-hungering to hear."

And then a Barron of County Donegal spoke: "Ye'll be after stopping and having first a sup o' tea." Cassie's hand, the one that did not hold the candle, closed over mine and drew me to the table. "Bless ye for coming, the both of ye; bless ye for coming this night."

The room we had entered was the kitchen. Cassie lifted an empty kettle off a cold stove and went out again. She crossed the hall; we heard her knocking at a neighbour's door. Mickey and I avoided each other's eyes. Irish hospitality held here in a New York tenement even as it held beyond on the moorland overlooking the sea; and again a grandchild of

Michael Barron had gone out to borrow food that the stranger within the door might be fed.

Neither Mickey nor I spoke. Our eyes searched every corner of the room for the poverty written there. No heat of any sort in the small flat. No gas. A deal table, two wooden-bottom chairs, a highchair, a few dishes in the corner cupboard. No sign of food anywhere. Across the room was stretched a line and on it hung a few garments, pitifully revealing: two thin little cotton shirts, two small pairs of black cotton stockings, well darned, a faded pink print dress, a well-washed pair of tiny blue cotton pants and the blue jumper that went with it.

Mickey spoke first, there was amazement in his voice: "I never went into a cabin in Ireland so bare. And not so much as a crumb left in the cupboard! Ye can see for yourself that the stove's as cold as a gander's nose. Aye, 'tis all true as the neighbour-woman said."

"There's a grocery store open at the corner." I took out "the bit of silver" Mickey had reminded me to bring and shoved it across the table to him. He put it in his pocket as Cassie returned. She brought in a steaming kettle; the other hand held a tray with sliced bread, a cup holding dry tea, a half-filled jar of jam, and a small end of butter. "The good tea. I'll have ye warm in a minute."

She steeped the tea. She spread the bread with butter and jam, and served us and then herself and worked to put a bit of merriment in all she did. "Now tell me—tell me all! Does Grandda look himself—does he still step out brave as any buchail across the moor? Is Delia as clever at making griddle bread? I mind the way it would taste with currants in it!"

And so I told of the summer, poured into her heart that for which she had hungered so long. She drank her tea but she ate no bread. Was she saving it for the morrow? Was she hoping to make a Christmas feast for the children out of it? Mickey pushed back his cup first and stood up. "Cassie, are ye minding that Saint Stephen's Day is coming, when the Wran Boys will be coming round in Ireland? And it's bad luck at every door that doesn't be opening to them, on every house that has nothing to offer them. Come on, lass, we'll be going out to see what can we find for the Wran Boys."

It was Mickey's way of saying celebration was at hand. The Wran Boys for Ireland are what the waits are in England; they go from door to door chanting their Song of the Wran and demanding hospitality. Cassie went without protest. I listened to their feet stumbling down the dark stairs. It was rare good fortune that Cassie lived in a neighbourhood where immediate necessity was the watchword and where shop-doors stood open to serve the eleventh-hour customer. I had said nothing to Mickey about toys for the children; but I counted on his training as postboy to meet all emergencies. Thinking of the children, I opened the second door leading out of the kitchen and found them.

It was a small, dimly lighted bedroom, cold as Greenland. The light came from one half-burned candle; but I paid it no attention then. The two children were in one crib, curled up like kittens to keep warm. The empty cot beside the crib was stripped of all covers; everything had been put over the children, tucked snugly in to keep out the cold. I looked and wondered what Cassie had expected to do that night—no fire to sit by, no bed with covering to it.

Two piles of nondescript little garments were folded neatly on two small chairs. Two stubbed-out pairs of small shoes stood, toe to toe, beside the chairs. And then I turned my attention to the candle; I wanted to see better the faces of the sleeping children. I started to pick it up and stopped, for the candle wasn't just a candle. It was a small, flickering shaft of prayer—a petition burning through the bitter night to the All-Seeing Eyes, the All-Hearing Ears. I stooped to look closer at the plaster figure before which it stood. It was Saint Bridget.

Hard as I looked at Cassie's children, I could see no marking of misery on their faces. By some miracle of motherhood she had kept them strong, happy. Their cheeks were rounded, pink as thorn-bloom. Their lips curved to half-smiles. There were no hollows under their eyes. I knew if those fast-shuttered lids should lift I would see deep Irish eyes, blue as cornflowers. They were bonny children, as Michael Barron had said.

I took the candle back to Saint Bridget. I took one shoe of each pair and in them I put the gold pieces meant for Ole Jensen and our Negro laundress. Cheques would do very well for them. I put the shoes, toe to toe, on the chest beside Saint Bridget. The gift was hers—not mine.

Cassie, Mickey, and the grocery boy made gayer entrance

than Mickey and I had made. They were laden to the ears: coal, kindling, food, bundles. While Mickey laid and kindled the fire, Cassie and I put boxes and paper bags neatly in the cupboard. She sorted the bundles, leaving some to open on the table. And all the while we worked Cassie's lips sang little words of thanksgiving: "The good meal. The good butter and bread. The meat. The good milk. Food for today. Food for tomorrow. Aye, feel the good fire. The stove will be full and roaring this many a day!"

It was a miracle what that stove did for all of us and the room. Our tongues loosened. Security came in, unseen, and took her place at the table. The little garments on the line looked less pitiful. Cassie set the kettle again—for more tea. "We'll toast the bread, brown." Mickey found a jar of gooseberry jam on a top shelf and climbed a ladder to get it. "We'll be having that." She laughed liltingly this time, as if joy, long banished, had come back.

Cassie opened the bundles on the table slowly, as if removal of twine and paper was a sacrament. Each thing she held up for us to see. "The good wool! I'll be knitting sweaters for them to wear under their thin coats. Feel the good flannel. There is enough for two dresses for Maggie and two little suits for Tim. Stockings—six pairs of them. Mittens! Warm woollen caps to pull over their wee ears. The last time I had them out they cried with the frost in them."

Her arms dropped across the table; her eyes took in the wealth they guarded. I opened the toys, Mickey the candy and a few ornaments for a tiny tree. While we trimmed it

Cassie set the table afresh. We sat long, planning a better future for Cassie and the children. Under the glow of promise and the warming cheer of the fire Cassie's face lost much of its load of care and grew unbelievably young and fair again. She was all for tossing our cups and reading the fortune in the tea leaves when the bells of the Little Church of Saint Anthony rang out for the midnight Mass. We stood and bowed our heads as the Christmas Day rang in. Cassie tiptoed to the bedroom door and opened it, and beckoned us to the threshold. She pointed to the crib and then to the candle guttering in its holder.

"Ye mind the tale? Like as not Grandda told ye. I was telling the childher it again the night and Maggie said: 'If we light a candle to Saint Bridget, will she find her way to us as she did to the wee Lord?' " Cassie flung a hand across her eyes. Tears were running fast now that trouble was lifted. "Faith, the candle's done for. It's lighted her way—straight."

I can see Cassie's face still, as she stood at the head of the stairs, lighting us down. We were almost at the bottom when her farewell came: "When ye write home to Grandda, tell him we're doing brave. God and Mary go with ye!"

13. The Feast of Fools

A LEGEND FOR CANDLEMAS

A Christmas Glee

Sing lustily of Christmas Folly,
Sing of Ivy, Bay, and Holly,
Banish each his Melancholy,
And evermore be merry!

Turn the spit and boil the pudding,
Give to all who come a-gooding,
Loose the falcons from their hooding,
And evermore be merry!

Give Sir Yule Log doughty hewing,
Give Sir Mutton tasty stewing,
Give Sir Wassail goodly brewing,
And evermore be merry!

Now flows each cask and casket's treasure,
Time the lutes to dancing measure,
Heigh and ho for Christmas pleasure,
And evermore be merry!

13. The Feast of Fools

IT happened in this wise:

Never had England been more harassed, never had her King been more merry. There were constant wars abroad and dissension at home. Meat and drink this was to those who would have more land and more power.

It came upon a day in midsummer that the King had gone a-hawking; and finding the sport but poor he had sought shade in a near-by thicket. He rested there, regaling himself with food and good wine, when a ragged, unshod boy discovered him and stood brazenly before him in a great curiosity. Haply the King was in good humour. "Knowest thou who I am?"

"Aye, the King."

"Hast thou no knee to bend?"

"Aye, truly, to God, Mary, and Her Son."

"How camest thou here?"

"A-riding. Mine is a good steed." And he slapped his thighs proudly.

"Doth he carry thee well?"

"Aye, wherever I have a will to go, and without feed or grooming."

The King laughed with merriment. "Well spoken. But thou couldst take some grooming thyself—both as to person and manners. Hast never heard of addressing the King as 'Sire'?"

"No, Sire."

"Tell me, hast ever heard of a king whose crown was so fastened to his head that he could not take it off, nor could he sleep in it at night?"

"Sire, there is none such. For to sleep thus he would be a fool and not a king."

"By the rood, the boy hath a wit," the King roared, slapping his own thighs. "Boy, wouldst be a fool—a court fool?"

For once the boy was not so ready with his answer. He stood long, changing his weight from one lanky leg to another, scrutinizing the King with a shrewd, canny look. "I would be a wise fool, I have heard of such. But I would sell my wit to no man, nor would I cringe to any—not even to thee, Sire."

"An honest fool. Methought there were none such," and the King wagged his handsome head with satisfaction.

In this wise did the boy come into the King's service. He received grooming from many hands, for both his speech and his manner. The King would call him by no other name than Nonesuch; and in time he became chief jester at the court. None could buy his favour, none corrupt him.

And now the Christmas season was at hand. Again the dreaded pestilence swept the land. In London, in the crowded streets, men died like flies. The King with his court fled to Canterbury, hoping that by keeping neighbour with spiritual grace and open air he would escape the plague. At once a fat purse was dispatched to the Archbishop, a reminder that he was expected to keep all pestilential humours from the royal door.

Christmas lacked three days. The King sat at meat and, of a sudden, pounded the table for silence. "I know not whom to appoint Master of Revels for this season. Forsooth I am sick unto death of the old masques and games. Methinks if I have to look again upon the mumming of Saint George and the Dragon, hear the Turkish Knight slay his lines, I shall send the whole troupe to the headsman. God's blood! Have we no fresh and bubbling wit amongst us who can devise new entertainment, something to split the sides with laughter?" And he looked balefully down at the fool

Nonesuch crouched at his feet, his ass's ears lopped comically askew, his bauble tinkling softly.

Sir Hugh of Chester sprang to his feet, a man eager to win the King's favour and having little liking for the chief fool. "Sire, I have but been waiting Your Majesty's pleasure. Even now a dish is prepared, fit for a king. I prithee carve it with care, for it well may hold a cure for your discontent."

He clapped his hands, whereupon the serving men scuttled away, to return in a moment, four of them, bearing an enormous pie. Its girth was a good twelve feet; and the crust rose to a peak in the centre like an ancient barrow. The King's eyes danced with approval. Rising he drew his sword and with caution pricked the crust into quarters. Lifting the centre he peered inside with great curiosity. What he saw sent him rocking with silent mirth. "A dish fit for a king! Thou hast spoken truthfully, Hugh. Step forth, my pretty blackbird."

Out of the pie, with mincing manners, stepped a dwarf, in black hose and jerkin. He was wrinkled and warty, as ugly a piece of human flesh as one could wish to see. His ears were somewhat pointed and stood forth from his head, his mouth was puckered sourly, his small, wicked eyes darted about the table until they rested on the King. He made obeisance in three languages, that midget; and when the King bade him speak and tell if he knew aught of Christmas revels he answered at great length.

It seemed that in some of the French cities there had come about a custom to hold a Feast of Fools upon Christmas

Day, at which time, in the church, they said a Mass for asses. But whether it was in honour of Balaam's ass or the one which had brought the Virgin to Bethlehem, no one could rightly say. A fool was priest; all fools attended. It was rare good fun to sing Kyrie eleisons to an ass.

"We'll do 't!" shouted the King. "We'll put on motley—cooks and courtiers, stable boys and clergy shall caper together. 'Twill be a rare sight to see priests and monks run about with asses' ears, with one red and one yellow leg showing under their cassocks. Only he who once was a fool shall be wise. What think you, Nonesuch?" He winked at the fool, who had grown as solemn as Whitsuntide.

"I like it not, Sire. The birth of Our Lord is no day to play ass with. Let us keep it rightly, humbly and worshipfully, even as our fathers have."

"A pox upon thee for a fool!" The King stood; the sword was still in his hand, unsheathed. He touched the blade of it now upon the dwarf's shoulder. "Sir Dwarf, I proclaim thee Prince of Revels, Bishop of Unreason. This matter of a Feast of Fools lies now with thee."

For the three days between that night and Christmas, tailors and artisans were forced to work the clock around. The dwarf was given free rein with the King's treasury. Those of the Church not willing to put on motley and sport the fool's cap were taken in charge by the guard; while the Archbishop was made a prisoner in his own palace, let out only at midnight Christmas Eve to say the Mass. He tried to gain the King's ear to bring his mind to some sense, but the King would not see him. The fool moped through the days, following the King like a patient dog, pleading with him.

"Sire, ill will come of this!"

"I do humbly beseech thee to consider the enormity of this desecration against Christ and Church."

"If thou wouldst but listen!"

At last the King threatened him with death. "Thou hast lined thy mouth with bitter herbs, and thy tongue lolls like a whippet's. Begone."

On Christmas Day such a procession turned out as England had never seen at a Christmastide. The King played the ass, his body encased in a wooden shell covered with hide, a head with monstrous ears capping his own. He brayed and capered the length of the street to the church, leading the procession; while the dwarf, with bishop's robes turned inside out, with mitre and crosier, trotted at his heels. Following these came the court and half the clergy in revellers' guise. There was Jonah with a gaping whale; Abraham with two sacrificial goats; Moses with Pharaoh's daughter; Solomon with the Queen of Sheba and a retinue of slave-girls. There were devils and nuns and fools of every breed, capped with coxcombs and asses' ears.

Within the church the mad throng knelt in mock solemnity. The dwarf chanted the service, all doggerel, from a book held upside down. A choir of roisterers sang antiphons to all fools, to which the ass responded with a loud "Hee-haw, hee-haw!" The while the fool Nonesuch looked on with sad, bewildered eyes. For he loved his King and could not brook that he should bring himself to such a blasphemy. A terror such as he had never known now filled his soul. For God would not let this mockery, performed within His house and against the day of His only Son, pass unpunished. Like crazy, witless children loosed from school, the King and court capered. They knew not what they did.

The mockery went on. Saint Stephen's Day saw stones and rubbish put within the church boxes to pay for the Masses said for the men upon the sea. The Day of the Holy Innocents saw a travesty performed wherein all slain were fools. And so it went, down all the days of the Long Christmas.

The Eve of Candlemas was at hand, that time when all candles should be blessed to burn with light, with truth, with holiness throughout the coming year. It was also, so Nonesuch believed, the day when the Boy-Christ had gone to the temple to teach the elders, for so a pilgrim from Jerusalem had once told him. This Candlemas therefore seemed to the fool as holy a day as Christmas, and to have it desecrated was to him a peak of wickedness to this fools' holiday.

He sought the King out and found him in his closet, having a new ass's head fitted, the old one being too ragged to wear.

"What-ho, spoil-sport!" roared the King.

The fool dropped to one knee. "Sire, I have asked scant favour of thee during these years of service. Is it not so?"

"Of a truth."

"May I beg favour now—one favour and the last?"

"I can tell better when I have heard it."

The fool shook his close-cropped head. He wore no longer the cap, since all the court wore them. "I would have the favour granted first, then tell it. But since it needs must be so, then this I beg: that Your Majesty give over further foolishness; that you go as King and English gentleman this night to church."

"What has happened to thy wit, thy fun, sobersides? Methought thou wast the best jester in all of England. We but go to have our candles blessed that fools may prosper through the year, that wit and humour have a bright burning. What better grace could fall upon all England than to have folly reign here for a twelvemonth?" And when Nonesuch made no reply the King turned on him with a sudden kindling of wrath. "Thou hast a sour disposition, fool. Take it hence!"

Straightway went the fool to church and to pray. He knelt before the shrine of Saint Augustine, that good and early man who had founded Canterbury and served it as its first bishop. Words came slowly: "Come thyself, this night, good Saint," he prayed, "or else send thou thy messenger. Thou hast loved this church even as I have loved my King. Therefore I do beseech thee to send some cure for this sore malady of foolishness which hath beset both King and Church. And have mercy upon all fools!"

He remained bowed, lost in silent prayer, so he did not mark the entrance of the King and court into the church. They came bedraggled, for they had worn their motley hard during the long days of Christmas. They came with drooping spirits, forced too long to antics. They came with candles ready to be blessed; so moved they down the nave towards the chancel where the mock dwarf-bishop waited to consecrate all with ale from a great flagon.

Made weary with sorrow and frustration, the fool rose from his praying and stood with back to wall, watching the procession. What strength had prayer beside the whim of a sovereign king? When the ears of earthly power refused to hear, how could one expect the Almighty ears of God or His heavenly attendants to open to the cry of a poor fool?

He watched, then saw with wonder the miracle take place. From out the shadow of the altar stepped a black figure, cowled. In the dim light his face could not be seen, but he was lean, gaunt, with the look of the sepulchre about him. The first to reach the steps cowered, while the dwarf-bishop took to his heels and ran down steps and aisle as if the Devil himself gave chase. As by some will stronger than his own, the first, who wore his ass's ear with poor effrontery, raised his candle for the blessing. Then it was that Nonesuch saw the monk, for so he looked, hold forth a cup and dip his fingers within to make the sign of the cross above the wick. In stentorian voice he gave the strangest blessing ever spoken at Candlemas: "May this candle bear light so long as the bearer is worthy of life. Amen!"

On the instant a flame sprang to the wick without aid of flint or taper. As the first fool courtier passed, the second took his place; and again the blessing rang through the vaulted church: "May this candle bear light so long as the bearer is worthy of life!"

What being, living or dead, had taken the Archbishop's rightful place? Voices hushed, then filled with horror and rose, while those who bore their lighted candles with shaking hands passed on and on. For even as each stepped away from the chancel, the wax began to drip with frightening haste and the candles to grow shorter, with every step taken.

"It is Pestilence itself who comes for us!"

"We shall not live to reach the doorway of the church!"

"The Black Death has us! God save us!" they whispered.

But Nonesuch the fool knew this was not so. He bore down through the frightened crowd. He reached the steps. He shouted to King and court: "Have faith, have faith! Can you not see, it is the good Saint Augustine, who has come to purge his church of your folly and lay a penance upon you?" And even as the fool bared his own faith the figure threw back the cowl and bared his face, showing the features of Augustine, monk, bishop, and saint.

"It shall be as the fool hath said. Ye men of folly shall make the pilgrimage to Jerusalem. Ye shall carry your swords for Christ and the faith. Ye women shall fast and pray and give your lives to acts of mercy until your men return. Let ye bear your candles, trimmed and with unwavering light, through the year to come." So spoke the saint.

And so it came to pass. The King led his court on its pilgrimage, and the fool reigned in his stead, a wise and just fool, beloved by all. But never was that Candlemas forgot. And when grandsires told the children of that Feast of Fools, they spoke with bated breath.